MY
LIFE
IN
THIRTY SEVEN
THERAPIES

RedDoor

KAY
HUTCHISON

MY LIFE IN THIRTY SEVEN THERAPIES

FROM YOGA TO HYPNOSIS
AND WHY VOODOO
IS NEVER THE ANSWER

Published by RedDoor
www.reddoorpublishing.com

The right of Kay Hutchison to be identified as author of this Work has been asserted
by her in accordance with sections 77 and 78 of the Copyright, Designs and Patents
Act 1988

ISBN 978-1-910453-77-3

Although the author and publisher have made every effort to ensure that the
information in this book was correct at press time, the author and publisher do
not assume and hereby disclaim any liability to any party for any loss, damage, or
disruption caused by errors or omissions, whether such errors or omissions result
from negligence, accident, or any other cause. In some instances the author has changed
the names of individuals and some identifying characteristics

This book is an account of one person's personal experience. It is not a
recommendation about the suitability or effectiveness of any particular therapy and
therefore should not be used to replace medical, or other professional advice. If in
doubt, always consult your doctor before trying any therapies

Every effort has been made to trace copyright holders and to obtain their permission
for the use of copyright material. The author apologises for any errors or omissions
and would be grateful if notified of any corrections that should be incorporated in
future reprints or editions of this book

A CIP catalogue record for this book is available from the British Library

Cover design: Liron Gilenberg
www.ironicitalics.com

Typesetting: Megan Sheer
www.sheerdesignandtypesetting

Print and bound in Denmark by Nørhaven

PROLOGUE

I'm sitting in a field of wild lupins. I'm six years old. The flowers are higher than me, hiding me, as sunlight filters through the gaps between the stems, warming my cheeks. It's very quiet in here, crouched inside my secret safe place, alone with my breathing as I watch the insects. A ladybird flies in and makes its way towards me and I admire its tiny beauty. I can hear children's happy voices in the distance and a robin singing.

Earlier on, my brother and his friend had chased me, brandishing lupin spears, which they threw at me. They had pulled each lupin from the earth one by one, ripping off the leaves in a great violent sweep but leaving the tapering purple flowers in a bunch like a giant arrow. They ran about like javelin-throwers and, when I tried to get away, launched them at me, laughing as they chased their small, fast-moving target, fair hair flying.

Eventually I'd managed to escape.

I hid in the lupins and they lost interest as the fearful shrieks died down and they moved on to their next battle somewhere else in the grounds of the Masonic Lodge.

卌 卌 卌 卌 卌 卌 卌 ||

1

'For some inexplicable reason, all I could think about was a desire to be somewhere else, on my own, away from everything'

It was the morning after the Grand Prix and a beautiful, sunny South of France day was emerging from the burnt rubber, dust and deafening noise of the previous day's race. The skies were clear blue and the 'ocean view' – as the hotels like to call the Mediterranean when they are selling rooms with a view at double the price – was filled with yachts and sailing ships tacking in the choppy waters. Most of the luxury crafts had approached the harbour and moored for only a brief stay during the race, but those that had remained overnight were beginning to cast off, passengers slightly the worse for wear but nonetheless continuing merrily on their way to St Tropez, the next stop on their trip along the coast.

Something was not right.

I looked across at Jonathan, my partner of twenty years. For some inexplicable reason, all I could think about was a desire to be somewhere else, on my own, away from everything. But Jonathan had arranged a special treat. He had booked us into a new boutique hotel in Nice to round off the Côte d'Azur trip.

Our trip to the South of France had become an annual highlight. The excitement of the week-long excursion included the build-up to the race, the practice sessions, watching the Ferraris come and go outside the Monte Carlo Casino, lunch at the Louis XV restaurant at the Hôtel de Paris, the fundraising charity events with guest racing drivers and the classic car auctions. There was shopping to look forward to – perhaps a new Louis Vuitton handbag, Hermès scarf or bottle of perfume, drives along the Moyenne Corniche to La Turbie, art exhibitions, bright sunshine and delicious food.

Each year we would get to know the drill a little better so that by now, Jonathan had it down to a fine art: where to go, when to book (the hotel was usually sorted at least six months beforehand – paying the exorbitantly inflated Grand Prix rates in advance in full); which restaurants were the best for seafood, truffles, steaks, for atmosphere or the people who went there (occasionally the racing teams would be at the table next to us). Again it was essential to book in advance (at least three months) to ensure that favourite table for two overlooking Villefranche-sur-Mer or that balcony up at Eze overlooking the twinkling lights down below was secured.

We stayed at the best hotels – Château Eza, La Chèvre d'Or or Loews – with incredible food and breathtaking coastal views to wake up to each morning with warm croissants and generous bowls of café au lait. We knew how to get invitations to le Bal des Pilotes at Le Sporting – the Grand

Prix ball was a special event with fireworks and a grand 'ahhhh' from the assembled guests (well, just the new ones) as the vast roof opened up to reveal the starry night sky.

One year we found ourselves in conversation with fellow Scot Jackie Stewart, who we had first met at a previous Grand Prix in Japan. David Coulthard and I accidentally bumped into each other on the crowded ballroom. Another year, preparing for an event, I had my hair done at the same time as Shirley Bassey and we chatted together as she had her tiny plaster-covered pinky expertly blow-dried by the salon owner after it had become damp during the wash.

Although we had both worked hard and made sacrifices along the way, being Scottish, Jonathan and I felt a little uncomfortable about our spending and having so much fun and didn't always think we deserved it.

As a couple, we were joined at the hip and happily codependent. And yet, in this, our tenth year at Monte Carlo, as we systematically worked our way through the carefully planned schedule, I began to feel a sense of dread.

I turned to my husband.

'I want to go home.'

Jonathan was reading his *International Herald Tribune*.

'I need to go home, Jonathan,' I tried again.

He looked up, slightly screwing up his nose as if to say, 'What's wrong with you?'

Then he put down his paper.

'What do you mean?'

'I want to go home – today,' I said.

'I don't understand, what's wrong? We've had a fantastic time and the hotel in Nice is booked – we can't just get up and go – besides, we can go and see your favourite exhibition at the Musée Marc Chagall and walk along the Promenade des Anglais, you love that.'

'I don't know what's wrong, but I'm going to go and pack and see if I can get an earlier flight.'

'Oh, for goodness sake ...'

He paused, looking over at me, and then, knowing it was pointless to argue, said wearily, 'OK, let me go and check if they have any flights. It will be difficult, you know this is the busiest day for people travelling back – that was the very point of us staying on and missing the hoards.'

'I mean just me. You stay on and enjoy yourself. In fact, I want to go home by myself. I'll go and ask the concierge about flights. You stay and finish your paper.'

I got up and left Jonathan sitting there, half-eaten croissant in his hand, a bewildered expression on his face as he watched me walk away.

And that was it.

That was the moment my twenty-year marriage ended.

How could something so special suddenly feel empty and meaningless? Did it start after the discovery of my husband's cancer, just weeks before my mother died? I had kept going, working even harder between trips to Scotland and caring for Jonathan back home. My mother's cancer lasted four years and she never recovered. Jonathan's was treatable and thankfully, after months of chemo and radiotherapy, he pulled through. But life was never the same, the worry, always there, hanging over us. You think about life differently.

卌 卌

We hoped everything would return to normal. But the experience changes you. Jonathan was a different person, more cautious, careful. And I changed too. You can no longer be happy-go-lucky and carefree. I stupidly tried to make up for my mother's loss, rushing around and for a while I tried to keep the family routines going, the holidays, the Christmas cheer, for my father especially. But it didn't really work and it didn't help. Everything became too much. I remember that feeling of desperation, wanting to escape. But as it turned out, it wouldn't be that simple.

2

'It was bound to be transformational, not to mention educational'

FIVE YEARS LATER

The driver was an old cowboy, moustached, in a stained cowboy hat with bullet holes and what looked like sawdust in his matted hair. He had low-slung side pockets full of bulging shapes and short, bow legs.

The only thing missing was a horse.

I'd found myself in Andalucía at a remote hilltop retreat with mountainous vistas, cactus and olive trees, dry hot sunshine and acres of time for peace and quiet. At the end of our two-hour yoga sessions (rooted in the teachings of Patanjali's eight-limb method), we would lie flat on our backs, legs and arms outstretched, star-like, winding down and surrendering to the sound of cicadas.

My friend Daisy had found the retreat. Frankly, by now, I thought I had seen it all, tried everything and was hopefully 'over', or at least coming to the end of, my very drawn-out midlife crisis.

I'd left my husband.

I'd fallen in love with a man who turned out to be married.

I'd lost my job.

I'd been on countless retreats and tried every therapy in the book.

Surely things would settle down soon.

Daisy, in her thirties, clearly relished the idea of this retreat. 'Do you fancy going with me? It will be very, very hot in July so you'll absolutely sizzle,' she had laughed delightedly. 'I know that's not your favourite thing but, on the plus side, there are loads of amazing treatments to make up for it – right up your street, and there's a pool (can't remember if you like swimming or not?). It's up in the mountains so shouldn't be tooooo bad for you. Looks gorgeous. Oh, and there's the healthy raw food for detoxing us, da'ling – all vegetarian, so good for me. And absolutely no drinking, which is good for, well, everyone, isn't it, especially me? I think, ha-ha,' she said nervously.

What a great friend to have, I thought, and I knew we'd have fun, we always did.

'Anyway,' she said, 'I've sent you the details so you can take a look for yourself, just need to fix up the dates – there's a big twin room with its own en suite that looks perfect for us and it's not taken yet, so take a look quickly da'ling, please can you, and let me know?'

Now the thing is I'm Scottish, and a Scot sizzling in the scorching sun when you've been brought up in the freezing rain just isn't a good combination. And I learned, when I was very young, that when you do finally venture out into the sun with your factor 500, well, it's pretty pointless, since all that happens is you turn beetroot, with burnt legs, a blotchy chest and red shoulder pads for about two days and then you revert to white – but this time with peeling skin. Great!

I'd be as uncomfortable and self-conscious as ever.

And of course there would be the usual parade of sun goddesses with their bronzed, toned bodies, lounging about the pool, looking perfect with flat tummies, great big Jackie O sunglasses and healthy drinks. Meanwhile, I'd be flapping about, flustered by the heat, hiding in the shadows or in my room with the shutters closed, air con on full blast, reading novels and eating melted chocolate bars that I'd sneaked in for emergencies. And you can't hide all that when you're sharing a room with the life and soul of the party!

̶H̶H̶ ̶H̶H̶

My first yoga holiday had been in Greece when I'd been on a fitness kick, exfoliating, buffing, moisturising and fake tanning every day. I had made a spur-of-the-moment decision to go to the retreat on a remote Greek island. I arrived with the most beautiful tan, a great big dollop of deep all-over spray tan from a salon the day before I left. A bit of a rigmarole with all the sleeping in dark-coloured clothing (!) to avoid staining the sheets (geez!), and not showering off the stickiness for at least twelve hours (eeewwww!). Anyway, after gently washing off the residue the next morning, as instructed, I felt much better when I saw – the perfect result – top tan – and it was really cheap too. Unfortunately, anyone who uses spray tan knows all too well that it's a job in itself, keeping it going, tending to it like some rare and delicate flower – you have to work at it.

Once on the island my spray tan immediately started to fade with the constant perspiring and regular showering to keep cool. Worse still, because I ended up hiding from the sun during the day, I wasn't building up a real tan underneath. Instead, I was rushing from shade to shade, under trees, restaurant awnings or sun umbrellas, or obsessively looking for a shop with air conditioning. Even at night, I couldn't escape the slow but steady loss of bronze shimmer – the heat was so oppressive that I had to lie awake with nothing on, tossing and turning, getting more and more agitated as I tried to duck the buzzing mosquitos.

By Day Three the fake tan had all but disappeared. Misery. I had imagined segueing seamlessly from fake to natural tan without anyone noticing. Sadly not. I must have been the only person – ever – to arrive on Day One with a great tan only to return home on Day Eight, lily white.

'Gosh, Kay, you look completely different!' said one of my fellow inmates, flicking through her holiday snaps on the plane back.

'Oh, let's have a look!' I said as she offered me her phone.

I'd arrived tanned, neat and tidy, but as I flicked through to the last pic taken just before we boarded, I could see the difference; although I was smiling and relaxed I was a total mess; ruddy face with shiny red cheeks, no tan. Without a hairdresser I had wild tousled hair and looked like a seventies hippy.

So, no, I wasn't rushing to say yes to Spain at the end of July. Daisy always took great pleasure in telling me how hot it was wherever she went.

Thirty-seven degrees in the shade today, wonderful, you'd die here, Kay! she'd text triumphantly.

She was a big traveller, always jetting off to hot places and sending me photos of idyllic hotels, clear blue sea, cocktails, champagne and empty bottles, I mean, empty beaches – she certainly knew how to live.

On the other hand, I knew it would be great fun and besides, it had been so long since I had been on a retreat that I was curious.

So it was then that, eight weeks later, I found myself in Spain in what turned out to be the hottest week of the year. We were twelve in total – eleven women plus the token man (fifty something with a ridiculously attractive twenty-four-year-old girlfriend). He was besotted and in awe of her yoga moves – as were we all. She also knew her 'powders' – her spirulina (in the morning) from her alkalisers and detoxifiers, hemp powders and super greens (later on).

The women were all going through 'women's stuff' – and it didn't matter whether they were English, Scottish, Welsh, Scandinavian, American, French, Colombian, German or Swiss, conversation seemed to focus on the same 'issues'. There were phone calls to partners, discussions about life, upbringing, work problems, eating disorders (mainly chocolate or wine) and plenty of laughter (sometimes tears) at mealtimes.

HH HH

Daisy hadn't made it.

Right at the last minute, she had been forced to pull out, leaving me to go alone. I was more than disappointed but on the positive side, I had a lovely room, big enough for two, all to myself, and it was a great opportunity to throw myself into the yoga, treatments and making new friends. There were lots of therapies to try, including something called sonic therapy, which I had deliberately left until the end of the week as a special treat to look forward to. Despite my musical background – instruments, orchestras, music degrees and working as a music producer for BBC World Service – I had never had sonic therapy. It was bound to be transformational, not to mention educational. I didn't know what to expect and the staff and regulars at the centre weren't giving anything away, except to say, 'Oooh,' and roll their eyes.

All I could do was wait and see.

The rest of the week was spent doing reflexology, massage, even the more unusual foot readings, swirling dervish dancing, biomagnetic pair therapy and the equally intriguing SCIO quantum feedback session which, thanks to the work of moon-bound NASA astronauts assesses physical data – your dietary intolerances, mineral deficiencies, organ imbalances, emotional symptoms – and then relates it to unresolved past events in your life. Wow. But, even despite all this, sonic therapy would prove to be the highlight.

3

'So many people in your life, Kay, have all been pushing their negativity towards you, offloading their issues and problems on to you, expecting you to help'

The villa was located ten miles away from the retreat hence the arrival of the ageing cowboy, my driver, in his bashed-up truck full of discarded water bottles, a jumble of crosses hooked on to his rear-view mirror jangling against the window. The road was heavily rutted with boulders, which he had to swerve to avoid. We drove in silence as I was tossed about until a villa perched on its own little mountain appeared in the distance. It looked important sitting there, blinding white with the sunlight bouncing off the walls.

He parked.

I got out of the truck and he pointed me towards the side of the villa.

'*Muchos gracias*,' I said before heading in through a wrought-iron gate and up the steps into the garden.

The shutters of the house were firmly closed. It was that strange time of day, siesta time, when Spain goes to sleep and everywhere seems to be deserted and tourists look lost, unaccustomed to having a hole in the middle of the day with nothing to fill it.

I approached the door and knocked gently, stepping back to wait, looking around at the incredible views across the valley.

When the door opened I was surprised to find a young woman, thirty-ish, petite with pleasing round features and soft brown hair pulled back neatly in a very long ponytail, before me. She wore a long white gown with turquoise satin tassels; she looked cool and comfortable and greeted me warmly.

'Hello, Kay, you made it, please come through,' she said as she turned and moved silently through the house.

I was shown into a large room, low-ceilinged with polished brown wooden furniture and fringed rugs and cushions. It was dominated by a row of large opalescent crystal bowls in various sizes, about fifteen of these giant opaque white 'mortars', arranged around the room in order of size. There were chimes, gongs, bells, brass bowls with Buddhist designs beaten into their surfaces and sets of tiny Tibetan brass cymbals.

Sam, the therapist, began to explain how she had come to live in this remote place and the benefits of sonic therapy. Our bodies and our cells are full of fluid, she explained, and the natural frequencies within them can be altered by sound. The therapy tackles problems by reducing 'dissonant' energy patterns that are 'out of tune' with the organism (you and me) and increasing good energy patterns, thereby creating harmony inside.

I loved this idea.

卌 卌

Music had always been a big part of my life. My mother had played the piano. She was especially good at 'The Dicky Bird Hop', which started everyone off singing.

'Ohhhhhhhh ...'

A very long 'Ohhhhh' in our family, as we sounded as if we were all just about to fall off a cliff waiting for the note to end, followed by a very fast staccato rendition, emphasising and enunciating every consonant of:

The chirruping of the birdies on the sycamore tree,
It's lovely to seeeee,
them having a spreeeeee,
they're lucky to beeeee,
so happy and freeeeee.

Then the verse:

Hopping about,
Skipping about,
Flopping about and
Nipping about,
the whole day through.

Mum would play the song on Grandma's tiny upright piano, one octave short of a full upright but a perfect scale and size for me aged seven. The piano lived in Gran's room at the front of our bungalow and I used to go in there whenever I could. I liked it in there. It was cosy and Gran used to give me grown-up cups of Camp Coffee, a brown thick liquid with chicory essence and lots of sugar that she diluted with water from the kettle, that I loved. She'd reach down to get the milk from under her bed (there were no fridges in those days, but it didn't matter as all the rooms were freezing cold). She would pour plenty of milk into the hot brown liquid to make sure it was nice and creamy. Then we'd sit silently sipping our drinks as I studied her antique treasures. There were all sorts of pictures, a Chinese tea set, hand-painted crystal vases from Venice with dancing Greek nymphs and a gold leaf mirror with a great eagle on top. I could see myself wherever I stood in the room. It was like an Aladdin's Cave.

I especially liked studying the Camp Coffee bottle – a brown glass bottle, tall, square-ish, with a romantic image of the Empire on the label. A big handsome Scottish kilted soldier in ceremonial military uniform had taken off his big furry hat to have his coffee. He'd placed his 'bearskin' down on the ground beside him and was drinking from a proper cup and saucer (very posh, pinkies in the air). He had plunked his big hairy legs wide apart, pushing the kilt down in the middle between his legs to hide anything untoward. The slim Indian man standing beside him had a moustache and was dressed in a turban and long cotton tunic. Obviously brewing coffee quickly for soldiers out camping was a very important job in those days. It was the world's first instant coffee, apparently.

After our coffee, Gran would encourage me to play her piano.

I played as best I could until finally one day, my mother, constantly pestered by me (and having had enough of 'Chopsticks'), gave in and set about finding me a piano teacher.

Miss Hodge was very old, but she was also inspirational and wise. She liked to meet her pupils first to ensure they had musical sensitivity and really wanted to play. She didn't want children whose mothers were pushing them into it, or who would prefer to be out playing in the streets. One evening, Mum dropped me off at Miss Hodge's house and I made my way through her kitchen and found her in her back garden for our 'interview' as agreed. She was bent over, tending to her flowers as she asked me a few questions. I was very chatty and, before long, she said she would be happy to take me for lessons and we could go and tell my mum. Soon afterwards, my musical life began in earnest.

Music, for me, was always about melody, harmony, the rhythm and mood, less about technique, so the scales and arpeggio practice was a challenge and slow. But, as soon as I caught the 'feel' of a new piece, I was off. I could throw the music away if I wanted to; I knew every rhythm and harmony and could visualise the musical notes on the page. My fingers took over, but more importantly, I was free to enjoy the expression of the music.

I began to compose my own tunes.

Playing the piano was now an escape, a special friend and constant companion. I played my favourite tunes over and over

again, happy in my own world. Once I'd found a piece that resonated, I immersed myself in it and played it for hours.

𝍲 𝍲

Back in Spain, in the villa, Sam asked about my life and
current health issues. We touched on the recurring problems
I had experienced in my relationships. After about twenty
minutes of gentle discussion, she paused and said, 'So many
people in your life, Kay, have all been pushing their negativity towards you, offloading their issues and problems on to
you, expecting you to help – and for all those years you have
accepted this without a complaint, you have absorbed their
woes, and helped them out at every turn.'

Whoah! Hang on a minute. Where did that come from?

I was about to respond but she carried on, 'And that man
that you loved so deeply, well, do you know that you saved
his marriage?'

I drew a deep breath.

A few years ago, this comment would have delivered a
painful blow – I would have wanted to lash out and deny this
terrible truth. It was the same feeling I had every time I
remembered the lovely moments we shared, walking in
Hyde Park, holding hands, laughing, bristling with the
excitement of being in love.

Instead the memories came flooding back and tears filled
my eyes as I recalled how it had all begun.

4

'It was thrilling, all-consuming, disorienting. But it felt like I was home when I was with him'

I'd spotted him on Day One. Sitting in the back row with my notebook, I could see his little bald patch. I took in the black trousers, really big shoes and a fresh white shirt. He was broad-shouldered and friendly with everyone. I thought it amusing that this big man's leg was shaking nervously. I found out later that it wasn't nervous fear; it was nervous energy, a need to get on – just like me.

The London Business School course comprised a group of fifty people, only four of which were women. We were there to attend a residential crash course in finance. We were being put up at a nearby hotel on Baker Street – the Sherlock Holmes hotel. Funny. There we were investigating financial models and problems, before walking past No. 221B on our way back to the Sherlock Holmes hotel.

My company was paying so I was determined to work hard. I wanted to do well. Each night I stayed up late working and then rose early to check my work again before going for a run to get some fresh air before the course started – once you were on the course, there was little time to yourself.

There were lots of bleary eyes at the start of the sessions each morning after everyone had been out on the town the night before. Who could blame them? They had been let out on their own, many from abroad. I slogged away quietly until the very last evening, when we all went out for a meal together and then on to a London club 'Cocoon', just off Piccadilly Circus, classy and heaving with people – he and I found ourselves chatting. He bought me a drink and suggested I avoid the Italian guy whom I'd been talking with earlier at dinner.

The following day, waiting to leave, we gathered together at the hotel, some of us still checking out. I'd ordered scones and tea – my 'well done' treat to myself. I was in no particular rush to take the short Tube ride back home to my flat, unlike others who were running for planes and trains. He came over to talk to me and I invited him to share my scones. He gave me his business card and asked for mine – I noticed his business card had 'Dr' before his name, slightly misaligned, as if it had been added as an afterthought.

He offered to accompany me back in his taxi en route to Paddington, where he was to catch the express to Heathrow for his BA flight home to Scotland.

Hard to believe that within a month we would be together.

He started emailing straight away.

I'd like to see where this could go, Kay, he wrote, to which I responded, surprised, curious, interested.

We tried to sort out a time. It would be weeks before he was back, but that only added to the excitement.

We need to be together, he said to me two weeks later.

I remember feeling happy, just like a little girl again. I felt cherished.

When he heard that I was meeting someone from the LBS group he messaged me: *Don't mention anything about us yet.*

How considerate of him to want to keep it quiet, in our little bubble, I thought.

̶H̶H̶ ̶H̶H̶

At the end of his training week in London, we booked the Oxo Tower, got all dressed up and he paid for a taxi from Notting Hill, chatting and canoodling in the back. Our table had a wonderful nighttime view over the Thames, bright London lights reflecting on the waves below. I went to wash my hands as we waited for our food and he texted me to hurry back after ten seconds: *Where are you? Hurry back, I'm missing you already.*

The people beside us looked on, and apparently said to him while I was gone, 'Ah, young love.' (Not *that* young!)

Another weekend we went to eat at Maggie Jones's – the favourite haunt of Princess Margaret and Antony Armstrong-Jones in the sixties, with its rustic wood, cosy booths and unfussy staff, just off Kensington High Street. We had walked there through the park in the warm evening sun. Just the place for couples wanting a quiet dinner away from it all.

One night, after having a drink at The Walmer Castle near Westbourne Grove, a work colleague told me he had seen us but daren't disturb us, as we'd been so completely absorbed in each other's company.

We stayed in a boutique hotel in Notting Hill.

Weeks flew by. The next time we met near the airport – he flew in so that we could be together and it was my turn to rush off the next morning to film a piece on the proposed legacy for the London Olympics.

One time, I drove down to the South Coast and the sleepy seaside town of Weymouth, where a specialist garage was adding yet more power and thrust to his matt black rocket of a car.

Congleton – another driving rendezvous; I drove up from London, this time, meeting him halfway, then we drove together in tandem for miles and miles until we found somewhere quiet to stay. Hours together before parting once again – tears and promises.

It was thrilling, all-consuming, disorienting. But it felt like I was home when I was with him. He was amazed at our incredible connection, 'It's either there or it isn't,' he told me.

He made me laugh.

'Eeek,' he texted when his travel arrangements suddenly changed.

'Don't panic, Captain Mainwaring,' he would say, adding to the fun.

He would lift me up and squeeze me so tightly, clutching

me and kissing me, all six foot four inches of him (me a slight five foot four inches and a half!). Once I had to say, 'Oi, everyone's looking, let me down, my dress is riding up!'

'Oh sorry!' he said smiling, gently placing me back down and helping me sort myself out.

He was my great big handsome Neanderthal, a dark, broad-shouldered, hairy-chested love with raw, almost primitive energy. I told him once, but he was not at all pleased. I thought of 'Neanderthal' as a kind of compliment. It was meant as a compliment. Oh dear. Here's the dictionary definition:

A Neanderthal man is an extinct species of human with a receding forehead and prominent brow ridges – uncivilised, unintelligent, uncouth.

You wouldn't want to cross him.

But he was also kind. At work there had been an accident and one of his team got injured. It worried him how the man's family would cope.

He brought me champagne.

He sent messages: *ILY*.

𝍷𝍷𝍷𝍷𝍷 𝍷𝍷𝍷𝍷𝍷

By now we had been seeing each other for nearly a year and, on this particular Friday night, he was late. I had been waiting for him for over an hour, checking my make-up, looking out the window, fluffing up the cushions, rearranging the white roses, tidying the bedroom covers (again), texting (no response) and I was so worked up and worried that something had happened, that he wouldn't make it.

I was getting very agitated.

It had been over a month since we had last seen each other.

I was about to scream in frustration when I heard a small knock on the door.

It couldn't be.

There had been no call, no text and I hadn't heard the doorbell or entryphone.

I gingerly opened the door and there he was. He had climbed (probably vaulted) over the 5ft iron gate at the front of the building and then, (don't know how), had managed to blag his way inside the block, run up the seven flights of stairs and surprise me.

He was laughing.

Soon I was laughing too.

When we eventually ventured out, we only had eyes for each other. We talked and talked. We were both into our work in a big way. He referred to himself as my 'Rufty tufty oilman'. He was fascinated by my travels. He told me how great I was and that I'd done really well in work.

I had to laugh when he sent me that photo of him on his new motorbike in a white T-shirt like James Dean, sitting proudly on his brand-new toy. He loved being free to take off whenever he wanted. He talked about his leathers and trips on the road (hmmm, you see there were warning signs, but I just didn't pay any attention – it wasn't my kind of thing).

I lovingly printed the photo and put it in the bottom of my drawer at home along with the group photo from the London Business School course where we first met.

But, it would all end in tears.

One day I would rip up that photo of him on his bike.

One day I would rip up the LBS group photo with him at the back and me at the front.

One day I would delete all his emails (amazing how difficult it is to erase someone completely, digitally, and I still haven't succeeded. He keeps popping up in the strangest of places).

But that wouldn't be for another two years.

5

'I was knickerless, braless, with a chain-smoking stranger about to stick pins in me'

I had block-booked the appointments the previous Saturday. It was cheaper that way and meant there was a plan, a schedule and an understanding on both sides. This wasn't a flash in the pan; it was serious. A course of six would be enough to see if it could change my life, both mentally and physically.

The Acupuncture Centre was situated in a parade of designer clothing shops in a fashionable square in Notting Hill. The shop, as you entered, was decked out, floor to ceiling, with images and descriptions of the plants and herbs on offer, remedies for this or that ailment, tinctures, teas and supplements that would solve any and all of your problems. There were Chinese tin tea caddies with airtight lids in bright red and gold. Some had images of pastoral scenes with Chinese figures strolling across bridges, through parks, in elegant *Hanfu* traditional dress. Most striking of all was the smell of the tea – today's special blend.

The Chinese receptionist, neatly suited in black, greeted me warmly, 'You very welcome, Miss Kay,' and, remembering me from the previous week, noted down that this was the first of my six appointments. 'You like wam tea?' she offered and, when I accepted, delicately poured two thimble-fuls of clear greenish liquid from an ornate china teapot into a tiny glass cup before disappearing to fetch the therapist.

The tea tasted a little odd but I sipped it politely and told myself that it added to the exotic feel of the place.

I was excited to try acupuncture for the first time.

I had a vague idea about what was involved and felt sure that this ancient Chinese cure would get right to the heart of my problems. The list was long. I was depressed, insecure, not sleeping, constantly nervy, out of sorts. I seemed to have lost my edge at work and no amount of extra effort could keep me ahead of the game – late evening finishes, weekend visits to the office just to make sure I had everything covered beautifully for the week ahead – all to no avail. Good, hard work had always sustained me in the past, but not now.

My closest friend seemed to know why things were going wrong and had tried to warn me as we sat together for our usual afternoon break in Crussh Juice Bar, sucking on our straws, she with her Green Goddess juice with added wheat-grass, me with my icy pink Love Juice smoothie with added fat burner super-booster.

'He's a c**k, Kay,' she said matter-of-factly. 'Some men just let you down, you can't trust them.'

At that, the tears started running down my cheeks, taking with them my carefully applied black mascara. I didn't want to hear it. I didn't believe it.

'But why is he not responding? We had such a wonderful time and it just seemed perfect. What should I do? I don't have the first idea how to deal with this. It feels very one-sided and the energy has disappeared as if he's found someone else. I'm confused.'

She put her hand on my arm, 'I feel bad for you, Kay – I hate seeing you this way. You're way too trusting and don't deserve any of it. You deserve much, much better. Because you've always had a decent man, all your life up until now, you've never had to deal with a c**k. I know it's difficult for you to see how someone can treat you like this but believe me, I've seen it many times before. You're not the first.'

My paper hankie was all black and soggy. My friend reached into her handbag and brought out a whole new packet.

'Here, have these,' she said sympathetically.

I was trembling – or was it shivering? – it was always cold in Crussh, what with the frozen drinks and the door left open to let in the fresh air.

'Do you want me to write a reply to him? Give me your phone and I'll do it for you.'

I nodded and blew my nose. I watched as she sat there drafting an appropriate response, straight and to the point. It seemed to take rather a long time but finally she sat back and handed over the phone.

'That should do it,' she said, 'and if he's serious, he'll get the message and snap right back into place.'

Gosh, it was pretty blunt.

I liked plain speaking but this was hard and final, not at all nice, which was normally my way. I never quite managed to say *how* disappointed I was or that I didn't think cancelling on me at the very last minute, yet again, was acceptable.

It was embarrassing, after telling all my friends at work that I was off on a short holiday with a great big smile on my face, then not going (again). I'd been really looking forward to our time together – such limited time – given that he worked abroad and 'home' was in the far north of Scotland. We only managed to see each other when he had the chance to travel through London or had work courses in London. I'd already taken the days off and you can't cancel, so faced an empty weekend, one of those Sahara Desert weekends – lots of thinking time but all the wrong kind of thinking. I was upset and angry too.

All the arrangements that I had set up and paid for were wasted.

And yes, of course he must go home to see his mother who had come down with a cold. She was the priority and he owed her a lot; bringing him up alone and giving him every chance in life through her own sacrifices, she sounded wonderful. But was he needed for the whole week, when we'd been planning this mini break for over a month? It seemed a bit odd.

Why was it always me that was let down?

No, I couldn't say any of that, couldn't ever say exactly what I thought. I didn't want to lose him.

That was the problem.

Since my divorce I'd read all the Venus and Mars books and *The Rules* and how you should behave and that being nice wasn't particularly helpful.

But it was a lot harder than I thought.

I was so annoyed at myself.

Had I learned nothing?

I wasn't sure I was ready to do this, but I knew that I was being given the best advice, from a good friend who not only cared about me but had experience, far more experience than me. I took a deep breath and pressed send... (ouch!)

〤〤 〤〤

So here I was at the acupuncturist's.

What on earth could they do with a wreck like me?

I drank my tea. Everything was furnished in red satin with gold threading. There was a tropical fish tank with some pretty coloured fish and soothing Chinese music in the background. I had allowed myself to sink into the very low squishy sofas, and so, when a white-coated Chinese lady came over, unsmiling, I struggled rather inelegantly to my feet.

'Oops, hello, are you the acupuncturist?' I said cheerily (daft question).

I quickly realised that the English-speaking part of my visit was over. The language barrier, in that moment, felt like a great wall between us. She didn't look at me but bowed her head slightly and motioned for me to follow her, into the basement.

Was that it?

I was hoping for some sort of description of what was to follow at the very least.

But I smiled obligingly and followed her into the basement with its bright fluorescent light. She lit a small candle in a minute stoneware dish. Then, using sign language, she directed me to take off my clothes and leave them on the chair, using her arms to indicate the 'casting off' of both bra and pants. Lots of nodding and encouraging sounds from us both.

It was cold lying on the bed and I was glad when she switched on a fan heater. The smell of fragranced oil from an infuser began to fill the room. Then came relaxing oriental music, with a gentle watery melody. I closed my eyes, transported to a peaceful faraway world. Maybe China?

She started with a gentle massage, the shoulders and legs – using tiger balm – that distinctive smell like Vick's Chest Rub that I remembered as a child. Sticky and medicinal.

Where were the needles?

I tried to relax as she started on the other side. Back and shoulders and backs of the legs, a brief foot and then head massage.

I heard her leave.

After a few minutes the door reopened and in came – someone else. There was the smell of cheap cigarette smoke tinged with body odour, and bad breath, as an inspection of my body began.

I lay in silence, trembling inside.

It quickly became clear that 'she' was now a 'he' as this presumably Chinese man darted about making grunting noises before lunging forward to hold up bits of my body, examining and then smoothing out the next bit of flesh. Having been lulled into a false sense of security by the massage, I realised that I was now in a basement room with a man I didn't know who was furiously opening noisy plastic packages each containing extremely long needles (I had opened my eyes for a quick look – and quickly closed them again).

I was knickerless, braless, with a chain-smoking stranger about to stick pins in me.

Yikes.

The first one (in my ankle!) hurt and I gave out a yelp. I heard him mutter a few incomprehensible phrases as he gestured for me to lay back down and be calm. (I can only assume that's what he meant, as he paid absolutely no attention to my startled expression.)

I opened one eye.

One sharp twitch and in it went, puncturing my scalp at the hairline. AAAAAAAA!

The other ankle got one, then the stomach (ooooooohh-hhh!), the wrist (eeeee!), the shoulder (aaaa!) and finally the back of my hand (ooow!).

Now I couldn't move.

He had me pinned down like Jack Black in *Gulliver's Travels*. Apparently his job was done, pins in place, because he went one last time around his work of art and promptly left the room.

It must have been a good twenty minutes that I lay there in suspended animation – if I moved, the needles scraped against my bones and I was beginning to feel pain. So I kept still. I tried not to fidget, listened to the music and waited. I daren't move my head with the needle embedded in my scalp. I looked about the room (luckily, no pins in my eyes), then shut my eyes again and tried to take my mind elsewhere.

6

'The physical act of inserting the needle would, I assumed, shock the system into action, or release trapped tensions, tensions that had built up over the decades'

Our family home was a neat, whitewashed bungalow set in the middle of an acre of ground. Along the perimeter was a high hedge. The bungalow was surrounded on all sides by lawn with several plane trees, two rowan trees, rose beds, a vegetable patch with potatoes and cabbages and some small, ancient pear trees.

Thanks to the hedge you couldn't see any of old Suzy's farm with her chicken coops or wooden hut.

Dad had made a swing by placing a large wooden plank between the forked upper branches of two trees and attaching some rope and a square wooden seat.

At the side of the house a gentle slope led to two rowan trees and well-tended rose beds.

On this particular summer day, Mum was rushing around as usual – my dad was away with work (he was an officer in the Merchant Navy), my grandma (Hutchison, my father's mother) was ill and staying in the front room and my grandma Hendry (Mum's mum) only came over to help out on Tuesdays when she brought the mince and on Fridays when she brought the fish. Mum had decided to put me out in the garden for some fresh air. I was ten months old and she had my older brother, now nearly three, to tend to.

I was good at amusing myself.

There I was, sitting in my pram on the path under the kitchen window. I was enjoying the feeling of sun on my face and the sounds of the garden. Until, that is, I realised I'd been forgotten. I now started playing one of my favourite games, which was to bounce up and down on the sturdy springs of the old-fashioned four-wheel Silver Cross pram. The pram was my trampoline. I was having a whale of a time, chortling away, convinced that someone would eventually take notice.

Alas no.

Instead, I bounced so hard that when I landed the brake was released and the pram began to move, ever so slowly at first, before picking up speed. Soon I was hurtling down the path at full pelt towards the privet hedge at the bottom.

As we (pram and I) finally hit the hedge, we parted company. The pram stopped dead and I was catapulted high up into the air, like a soft white ball of chiffon and silk, spinning around over the hedge and past the lawn, landing with a dull thud in the rose bed.

There was a moment of hush as birds, insects and local dogs froze.

Waiting.

A terrifying noise was then let loose as I realised what had happened. I let out a great tonsil-vibrating, 'WAAAHAH-HHHH, sob, sob, sob!'

It was the dog that found me.

Lassie came bounding up to me, wagging her tail enthusiastically, licking my ears and kissing me all over my face, trying to make it better.

꜀꜀꜀ ꜀꜀꜀

And now here I was waiting for the acupuncture needles to release trapped chi (energy), to get everything working again and flowing smoothly around my body, releasing any 'blockages'. The physical act of inserting the needle would, I assumed, shock the system into action, or release trapped tensions, tensions that had built up over the decades.

Lying in the semi-darkness, I had no choice but to surrender.

There was no 'talking it through'.

Should I have gone to an English-speaking or indeed English acupuncturist? It probably wouldn't have held the same fascination for me. The authenticity seemed important.

The acupuncture session came to an abrupt end.

My acupuncturist had arrived back and removed each pin swiftly, rubbed the needle site and threw the used needles in the bin. As soon as they were out, he left.

Not a word was said.

I got changed, went upstairs and waved to the receptionist, who was selling ginseng root to a customer.

She looked over: 'See yoo next tam, Miss Kay, you had lovely "tree-men", yes?'

I nodded and smiled.

Only five more to go.

7

'You must be patient. You can't rush things here. I know it looks confused right now but things will clear'

I was sitting on the sofa with a pen and paper to hand.

The mobile phone finally rang.

Click.

'You have paid for a twenty-minute call. Stay on the line to be put through to your chosen reader, pin number 0634. And remember, these calls are for entertainment purposes only ...'

That part always made me slightly uncomfortable.

What percentage of callers would actually do this for fun?

Regulars like me – and there were lots of us – weren't looking for a bit of fun. This was serious. I was desperate for help, desperate to know what was going to happen.

I pressed the number to accept the call and waited a few seconds.

Click.

'Hello?' I jumped in.

'Hello. Good evening, can you give me your name and date of birth, please?'

I'd stopped wondering why they needed this information and whether or not I should give it out a long time ago. It would probably just slow things down and you had to trust them.

'Thank you, Kay. I'm a natural clairvoyant and psychic reader and I use the crystal ball. I can read for you and guide you in whatever area of your life you need help – relationships, family, career. Have you spoken to me before?'

'Yes, a few months back. You gave me a very positive reading. I felt much better afterwards.'

There was a pause.

'OK. And how can I help you tonight, Kay?'

She had a strong Indian accent and spoke softly and slowly. I concentrated as hard as I could, shutting my eyes.

'I want to know what's going to happen with the man we spoke about before. Things are still not getting much better.'

'Ah yes, I can see that.'

Another pause.

Her mobile rang. *The Flintstones* theme tune 'We'll have a gay old time...' with some frantic shuffling and background noise.

Then it stopped.

'Oh, so sorry. Should have switched that off before we started. Let me see... The spirits are giving me some initials, letters of the alphabet – does the man have any of the letters ARPJD in his name?'

I wrote down the letters in case I forgot but knew immediately that all three men that had some influence in my life at the time were there – Jonathan my ex, an old friend and, of course, the man I was involved with who worked abroad.

'Yes.'

I tried to focus on the man I was calling about, putting other thoughts aside in case it affected the reading.

'Ah good. Well, I need to tell you that you mustn't worry, Kay. All will be well. The spirits are showing me this. And this man, the man of your destiny, he is younger than you by two to three years and he has dark hair? Is this correct? Is this the man you are thinking about?'

'Yes.'

Two of them had dark hair. Two of them were younger.

'Well, at the moment the man you are thinking about, he is quite troubled and very unsure on what to do. But he does love you and cares a great deal for you. He just needs to sort a few things out himself before things can get going properly again. And after that, all will be well. You will be happy.'

'That would be good,' I said, relieved. 'I was beginning to think I'd have to get out of this, that I should move on. But perhaps I should persevere. I would like it to work. How long will I have to wait?'

'I can't be absolutely sure of the exact timing but it shouldn't be too much longer. Perhaps four months at most. You must be patient. You can't rush things here. I know it looks confused right now but things will clear.'

'I'm finding it hard to be patient. It's been a long time already.'

'Yes, I understand that it's difficult and I see you want things to change so very much in your life. But if you really want things to happen, you have to go with the flow and let things happen naturally. You can't force it. If this is meant to be, it will happen. And you will be happy and contented, I can see that.'

'Can you see anything about my work? I'm keen to know if all the effort I'm putting in at the moment will lead to something and that I'll start to earn regularly again. I am living off my savings just now as it's mainly unpaid.'

'Why are you working for no money?'

'I've been working on a project important to me, something that I was working on before I was made redundant and that I was leading on behalf of a large number of companies. I feel responsible to them – and to myself – to continue. After I lost my job, I needed to continue to keep going for my own sanity and not to let anyone down. I had some redundancy money to keep me going and it's the type of thing I want to be doing in the future. It's important work... I hope it won't be like this for long.'

'You need to be paid for the work you do. And I can see that you will be. There is money coming and you will be rewarded for all your hard work and efforts. There's abundance coming. And you will be acknowledged for what you have done and, far more importantly...'

Click.

The line went silent.

'You are nearing the end of your reading You have two minutes left to finish your reading or you can extend your call. If you wish to continue the call after the two minutes, press 1. This will cost £1.20 per minute and will be charged to your credit card. If you wish to end the call, you have two minutes remaining to conclude your reading. I'm now returning you to the call. Enjoy the rest of your reading ...'

I didn't press 1.

I thought we had covered the important bits.

Click.

'Hello?'

'Hello, Kay. Is there anything else you want me to look at in the time we have left?'

'Perhaps my health? It's not so good with all the confusion going on. I'm having panic attacks, especially waking up alone at night. I used to be so together, but now I feel very low at times, a bit lost. Will that improve...?'

'Well, I'm not a doctor. I advise you to go to your doctor to get everything checked out – your blood, your circulation and you must eat properly and look after your health. But I can see that everything will resolve in time – change is coming and things will sort themselves out. You will be fine. Not to worry, Kay. You mustn't worry about things. Have you been to the doctor already?'

Click.

The line went dead.

8

'I'd taken to calling these mostly kindly, anonymous, people about my personal life. It was all hidden away'

'We're sorry but this number is no longer in service...'

I listened to the long, empty silence.

After three long, turbulent years, I'd been finally cut off.

It was like he had died.

I was angry, at everything, but especially at myself.

I hated myself for being stupid. So gullible.

He was already married.

I had always been against this. I should have realised, of course, and suddenly it all made sense – the cancelled visits, the delays. He was committed elsewhere and finally it was clear.

From every perspective, it now looked as if he'd never had any intention of making it work.

By then, I was in so deep that I found it hard to accept. I was still in love. There was a distancing for a while, but then he'd reconnect and each time my hopes were raised – 'he's free, we can be together'. He would tell me, 'I just need a little more time.'

He knew I was vulnerable. But still, he kept me dangling.

I found it impossible to let go and any sensible judgement was gone.

'It would be great to christen your new flat, Kay,' he texted, just as I was beginning to move on.

✻

We met at the airport that last time. We had intended to eat but, in the end, we didn't even have a glass of wine.

He looked older, greyer, strained.

I asked him straight, 'Are you still married and living together?'

'More or less,' he replied vaguely. I didn't understand.

Surely what we had counted for something, surely he was back because he realised he had got it wrong? I was so distraught that, in one last-ditch desperate attempt, I offered to move back to Scotland, look after his mother and give up my work, career, everything.

'But I have a life, Kay,' he said in response.

Yes, so do I. I'm a human being too, someone you've been close to, not some 'thing' that can be picked up and dropped when you feel like it, I thought, but didn't say.

I could never say what I really felt.

I'd played my last card.

As I retraced my steps along the long, dark corridors from the hotel back to the train the next day (he had left early to catch a flight), I felt bereft. There was no moving forward.

That was the last time I saw him.

Shortly after that, he disappeared into thin air.

Later that day I called a psychic.

I didn't want to burden my friends.

My ex-husband was worried. Through all the ups and downs of our years together – first love, careers, long separations caused by work, the difficult aftermath of cancer that pushed us apart and forced us to question our lives and the choices we made – we were always good friends, and even after the divorce, although we knew there was no going back, we were still in contact. He sensed something was wrong, but I didn't want to share this with him. He would find it difficult to understand why any of this was happening. He wouldn't recognise me as his former wife.

I was a different person now.

I had fallen in love.

卅卅

Not only that, it had turned out badly.

When later that month my credit card bill arrived, I was somewhat horrified to see how many calls to psychics were listed. Once upon a time I'd happily spent my money on socialising – those holidays to France, restaurants, gifts, new clothes or flights home to Scotland to see family. But that had all changed.

It showed how isolated I'd become. I hadn't talked to anyone close about my problems. Instead I'd taken to calling these mostly kindly, anonymous people about my personal life. It was all hidden away.

'Hello, am I speaking to Kay?'

'Yes.'

'It's Shivana here, how can I help you today?'

'I just want to know what's going to happen – I'm feeling pretty low just now...'

'Not to worry, Kay, we will find out. Are you interested in knowing about your career or is it your relationships? Shall we look at relationships first?'

'Yes, that would be good.'

'Well, I see the man of your destiny has the initials ARPJD in his name.'

I took a deep breath.

9

'Imagine hundreds of glasses and not just high-pitched but low-pitched too — combined with deeper tones, a whole orchestra of sound'

The sonic therapist had brought everything tumbling back. But this time I didn't feel the punch. I just felt sadness. As Sam spoke to me, I wondered how she could have known so much.

'He forced all his issues on you, you absorbed them into your life, you comforted him and made him think. You also opened his eyes and made him appreciate all that he had, all that he might lose, all that he had been ignoring in his life for so long.'

It was so hurtful to hear her explain that I was a pawn in the grand scheme of things.

She continued, 'But now, it's time to stop letting this happen, letting people send you their negative energy. You need to get on with your own life and leave them behind with their problems; they're not yours, so just gently hand them back and start paying more attention to yourself and take responsibility for yourself, for your future. It's great that you are taking things into your own hands and coming on retreats like this. It's healing and restorative and you're doing it for you, no one else. You have a great time ahead of you, now that you are ready to make this change.'

Guided by Sam, I moved over to the centre of the room, close to the crystal singing bowls, and laid down, breathing deeply at first, and then, when she told me to settle down, my breaths became quiet, less deliberate, with a more natural rhythm as I began to relax.

I shut my eyes and let my thoughts drift.

Soon, out of the silence came an unearthly sound – it was the tiniest sound at first, continuous, with bell-like depth. I felt the vibration deep in my chest before spreading to other parts of my body, my stomach and the front of my head. It was a strange feeling. Just a single sound at first, pulsating. Soon I was conscious of other notes being added slowly, one by one, overtones, other harmonics, the whole sound vibrating through and across my body, powerful and deeply comforting.

It reminded me of the sound made when someone runs their finger round the rim of a crystal glass. Imagine hundreds of glasses and not just high-pitched but low-pitched too – combined with deeper tones, a whole orchestra of sound.

Occasionally, weird scraping noises would emerge then disappear.

And then finally, the last, but most unexpected addition to the 'symphony' was a human voice, not obvious at first, with all the other sounds in play, but gradually, emerging, clear and distinct. It was Sam adding her unique vocals to the ensemble.

I lay there, completely absorbed by the experience. The physical sensation was oddly calming. Now I knew why no one had said anything about the treatment; it was impossible to capture the feeling fully in words.

ℍℍ ℍℍ

Back in London, Daisy rang for a gossip.

'How did it go, da'ling? Any good stories? Were the treatments amazing? Was the food awful? Was it too hot for you?' She laughed, obviously hoping the answer to all of the above would be yes.

There was so much to say but somehow all I could manage was, 'Unbelievable treatments and the food was great, but it was very hot, and I really wish you'd been there too. Let's do something else together, but perhaps next time we'll avoid the no-alcohol retreats. Otherwise I'll be on my own again.'

'Sound advice,' she said.

10

'It felt good. It made me think differently about my predicament. There was no blame'

One of my oldest friends, a work colleague from my early days in London, recommended her therapist after I'd arrived on her doorstep late one evening, rung the bell and burst into tears as soon as she opened the door.

'Oh, Kay, what's wrong?' she said.

After ushering me into her living room and pouring me a glass of wine, she said it was no use being prodded and having needles stuck into me if I didn't go and talk to someone.

'You need to talk to someone who can deal with this properly – a professional who understands what's going on.'

So it was, then, that a week later I found myself outside a house on the main road between Shepherd's Bush and Chiswick. When the door opened, I was surprised to find an attractive woman with bright red lipstick and shoulder-length raven hair with a striking grey streak smiling at me.

This was Anna, the psychotherapist who had come so highly recommended.

Extremely well spoken, which gave me confidence, she was clearly educated and intelligent – someone you could learn from.

I warmed to her soft, measured tone.

She hung up my coat and led me through her home past Peruvian weavings, Iranian rugs, interesting stone sculptures of rotund faceless figures sitting entwined on a block, small modern paintings with lots of splashes of colour, shelves and shelves of books, crystals, wall hangings and carved wooden chests. Light flooded in from the large windows.

We sat down opposite each other at the far end of the room in a small alcove with bright yellow walls and a view looking out across a pretty garden. The chairs were small and low, old-fashioned but comfortable.

It was quiet.

I was nervous.

Anna was formal and firm in her delivery. She did not ask me to fill in a form (something which I later discovered is quite common in other counselling sessions). Instead, she started straight away by asking me to tell her what was on my mind today.

I began to relate my story, why I was unsettled and lacking in direction, what was troubling me at work and in my personal relationships.

I felt happy to talk.

Anna asked me to explain why I thought things were as they were. She asked me what I thought I should do. At every opportunity, rather than questioning what I said, she accepted how I was feeling and she was sympathetic. It felt good. It made me think differently about my predicament. There was no blame.

This became the first of our hour-long sessions, which always ended with Anna saying gently, 'Well, that's us coming to the end of our session now, Kay.'

I admired her ability to take advantage of a natural pause in our exchange and say, 'Let me go in and see what's going on.'

I would watch her shut her eyes then start to describe a scene to me. These 'visualisations' lasted a few minutes. She described everything in detail. Sometimes she seemed surprised with what came up and laughed, sometimes she was shocked and sad for me.

We agreed that I would come back the following week for the second session.

卌 卌

Six months in, now accustomed to the routine, I sat as Anna described seeing me as a young girl standing in a deeply furrowed field.

'I see you, Kay, with both feet stuck deep in the mud – enormous ploughed-up folds with great furls of dark, drenched mud. You are clearly finding it impossible to move forward out of this mud – it's as if you're trapped in thick, dark treacle and you can't even shift your legs.'

She paused, eyes still closed, the sides of her mouth twitching slightly as if experiencing it for herself.

'Now I see you reach down, behind you, Kay, and you're trying to lift up something very heavy.'

She spoke carefully, as if examining the scene in forensic detail. 'It's some sort of tool with a long wooden handle.' She paused. 'Oh, it's an axe, Kay, and now, look, you're trying to steady yourself in that deep mud so that you can grip it properly. And slowly, ever so carefully, you start to lift this extremely heavy object and you swing it away, back and then up, right over your shoulder. And, although you are small and it's really very heavy, and your face is strained, you're determined to and you manage, you manage to throw it up with all your might. It soars into the sky and comes down to land right across on the far side of the field, smashing into the roof of a house. It shatters the tiles and leaves a huge hole and now the people in the house have all come running out; they're screaming and running around down below.'

The clock chimed.

I looked around and waited, nervously, wondering what would happen next. A few moments later, in the silence, Anna, head slightly bent downwards for the past ten minutes, straightened herself up in the chair, composed herself, then gently opened her eyes and looked across at me.

'Well,' she said, 'that's a pretty striking image they're giving me, Kay.'

I smiled uneasily.

'But what does it mean to you, what comes to mind?'

I had been fascinated by the image but hadn't really thought how to explain what it meant, now back in the hot seat. And yet, I immediately thought of something and began to talk. Was it a description of me as a child, often stuck, often feeling unable to express myself, misunderstood and somehow kept down by others?

'I think it's me at home when I was small,' I said. 'Perhaps I'm now getting my revenge?' I laughed.

'There seemed to be a lot of anger there, Kay,' said Anna seriously.

'Perhaps it means I've been kept in my place all these years and it's now time for me to express myself and say what I really think, even if it's shocking?'

As a girl, I remember feeling small. I was the youngest, regularly the butt of my family's jokes, often discouraged from speaking out – which was unfortunate, as I often did speak out. I couldn't help it. It was my nature. That is, until it was knocked out of me.

'That's not the way to make custard,' I once said to my grandfather, who was busily making a pot of yellow lumps in the kitchen. 'That's not the way my mummy makes custard.' After seeing the look in his eyes, that silent glare, I knew at once my views were not welcome.

Other comments were stifling.

'Get back in the kitchen where you belong,' was one of my father's lines.

Or, 'I've got bigger pimples on the back of my hand,' when I had to ask for my first bra after a (far too) close encounter at school, preparing for the school dance.

The phrases 'good child-bearing hips' or 'lovely, shapely legs' followed me around, usually said out loud and, even worse, when my parents had company.

I wanted to run away.

11

'My nightmares were always about falling, spinning down into a great black hole'

'Tell me a little more about your home when you were growing up, Kay,' said Anna.

In a flash, I found myself back in the gloomy hallway with the leg crashing through the ceiling.

I remembered cold nights, a solitary street light flickering, branches forcing themselves against the window in the howling wind, giant leaves like eerie hands waving about in the dark, the animal carcass in the bathroom, the rodent (a 'clawed jird') scraping about on my bedroom floor, the dead dog, the nightmares and falling, the angry man in his cap stirring away in the kitchen, the grey-haired old woman boiling up a kettle in her bedroom, the 'sick-bed' room and the child-trap behind our heavy front door.

This was home.

And yet, looking back, it had been a happy place to grow up in. It was the place I came back to after school or Brownies − us wee girls in brown outfits, yellow scarfs, woggles and berets learning how to knit in the church hall. Our lounge was sunny and inviting with comfy seats. Not too comfy, mind you, with upholstered chairs in dark red, carpet-like material and a wispy white fleck pattern. This was where the family congregated – ate together, laughed together, watched TV. Behind it was the kitchenette with a sink, cooker and the yellow and blue kitchen cabinet with its middle door that pulled down to become a work surface and all its interesting little compartments, for plates, pots, chopping and working.

卌 卌

'What else can you see?'

I'm standing in the hallway on a large pink carpet with swirly cream and leaf-green designs at the edge. There's a big heavy chest of drawers to the right with large round brass handles. I can see my mother's leg dangling from the ceiling.

I burst into tears. Covered in plaster dust from the hole she's just made when she slipped in the loft, I call out her name.

'Mum!'

She laughed even though it must have been a shock, not to mention expensive.

Dad was always away 'deep sea', sailing the oceans of the world, so she had to do things herself, like fetching heavy things from the attic.

Then there was the dead animal in the bathroom.

Once a year, for a week, we wouldn't be able to use the bath. A close friend of my father's, a New Zealander whom he had met working on the big tankers sailing around the world, would send a whole frozen lamb. Without a fridge, we made do with the bath. The carcass lay there, slowly defrosting as it was chopped and sliced into various pieces for everyone to enjoy – uncles, aunts, grans and grandpas, old Suzy up at the farm, friends, neighbours and assorted extended family meat eaters.

卌 卌

My brother was called Glenn.

Glenn's room was special. At the back of the bungalow, it was light and airy with a large window facing out on to the back garden. It had cream-coloured curtains and lots of interesting things for me to look at – books (he was studious and clever), Corgi cars, Dinky Toys and lead soldiers. I loved my big brother. When I had nightmares, I'd creep into his room in the pitch-black and approach his bed.

'Glenn… I've had a bad dream, can I come in, please?'

He'd ruffle his sheets and half sit up, disoriented, finally moving over. 'Oh, I suppose so,' he'd reply, making room for his annoying little sister.

I'd soon fall asleep.

My own room, in contrast, was crowded with tall dark furniture, a beige and brown tiled fireplace with a fire that was never lit.

Once, late at night, getting out of bed, I trod on something furry. It squeaked and scuttled away, its claws scraping the floor as it dashed off and I quickly jumped back into bed. I never did that again without slippers and without turning the light on first.

My nightmares were always about falling, spinning down into a great black hole.

卌 卌

'Tell me something happy that you remember, Kay.'

'One summer, the school gerbil came home to stay and I had to look after him every day, cleaning out his nest, changing his water and pumpkin seeds. He was good company. His cage was placed high up on the tall chest of drawers and as I lay in my bed I could hear sweet little noises, tiny scraping sounds, murmurings, shuffling, straw being moved around as it made and remade its cosy bed. At the end of the summer, he died. I was distraught, inconsolable...'

'It's not your fault,' Mum said.

But it must be my fault; who else was to blame?

The loveliest room in the house was Mum and Dad's pink bedroom. I was only allowed into their room on special occasions, when I was ill.

Being ill meant Mum had to take time off work and travel home during her lunch break to give me something to eat. So I was only off school when I was really unwell – and I almost always had perfect attendance – the (only) gold star on that line in my report card.

She would come in with a bowl of hot soup. I'd eat it and then she'd come back in to collect the bowl when I rang a small silver hand bell and disappear to leave me to recover. All alone.

On the big bed, with its beautiful pink satin cover to match the curtains − ornate Victorian mirror patterns embroidered on its surface in white − I'd enjoy the view. It was sumptuous, all this light, all this space, all this pinkness with lovely swirly patterned white net curtains and light wooden wardrobes with a dressing table and chair.

⫶⫶

My father decided to redecorate my room in wild horsey wallpaper. I'd begged and begged for a horse or a pony. I said I would look after it myself, 'We can keep it in the garage under the swallows' nests, Mum.'

But of course I couldn't have my own pony so, instead, my parents went to the trouble of redoing my room in lovely horsey wallpaper. Black and brown horses galloping, rearing up, swishing their tails, wild and free, against a stark white background.

My dad was a great wallpaper-er and spent hours carefully preparing the room, mixing the jelly-like paste, laying out the broad strips, cutting, pasting and folding paste-to-paste surfaces so as not to crease the paper, carefully matching the design and fitting the edges together with the greatest of care. He took pride in his work. Only this time there had been an issue with the size of the walls vis-à-vis the breadth of the rolls of paper and he ended up with a problem at one corner. He came up with a cunning plan and, instead of adding a tiny piece right in the corner, he carefully smoothed off the edge, leaving a curved corner with matching horse pattern and no need for a tiny fiddly little strip to fill the join.

Once it dried and I was back in my 'new' room, all smelling lovely from the paste and fresh skirting board paint, I found myself fascinated by that smooth curve around the corner. I began to make a trail of teeny holes all the way up the wall. The corner was beside my pillow so it was easy for me to lie there and pop a couple more in. When I could no longer make the perforations in places I could easily reach from a lying down position, I proceeded to sit up on the bed and then stand up to continue the pattern up the wall. Once I had completed that, I went to get a chair.

My father arrived home a few weeks later. All his hard graft, care, expense and pride, and here was this little besom (as he would refer to me when not pleased) ruining it all. Oh dear. Once I started, I just couldn't stop and I did, all the way up to the ceiling. It was my room after all and I didn't really see what the problem was.

'Ach, Kay, why did you do that?' my mother said.

I was in the bad books.

Then came the summer holidays.

Lassie had puppies, six of them.

But, we were due to leave that day, and now came the news that we were only allowed to keep one pup for Lassie. My grandfather had filled an old enamel bucket with water and, one by one, the perfectly tiny, helpless sleeping bundles went in.

I burst out crying uncontrollably and later complained, eyes still streaming with tears, 'Why couldn't we take them all? Why would we do that just for a silly holiday? Why couldn't we find homes for them? Brenda and Cecilia would love a puppy and were always round stroking Lassie!'

Then 'I don't want to go on holiday now – we could have gone on holiday another day.'

But a girl wasn't allowed to have opinions. The men knew best.

༜༜ ༜༜

Here, Anna stopped me.

'Well, all that putting you down must have led to a very strong will,' she said.

'Probably,' I nodded.

She was right.

This was the first time I had ever really begun to think of things this way. It had never occurred to me.

I'd just swallowed it, hidden it and tried to forget about it.

As it turned out the puppy we had chosen for Lassie didn't last long. Glenn had been given the honour of choosing his favourite – it was light brown, like Galaxy chocolate. He decided to call him Zorro as he had a white mark on his forehead that looked like the 'Z' of Zorro, the dashing outlaw from the TV series, the cunning hero.

But soon Zorro wasn't well and I noticed the adults looking at each other with worried faces as we all tried to rally the little bundle. We wrapped him up in a big cosy hand-knitted jumper and sat him next to the fireplace which, when we went to bed, was still very warm. Lassie had licked the pup quite a lot during the day but, for some reason, she had stopped and didn't seem to want to be with him after a while so he just sat there on the hearth alone in his big jumper, sleeping and not moving.

When I woke up the next day, I jumped out of bed and ran into the living room, desperate to see our new pup. But he was just a little limp cold thing, lying there in that jumper. There were only grey and black ashes in the fireplace now.

I picked Zorro up and cuddled him. I went in to get Glenn and blubbed, wordless wailing. Glenn didn't cry: he was a boy and boys were not supposed to cry.

But I knew he was crying inside.

12

'there was to be no physical contact (between anyone), no drinking, no yoga, no jogging, no smoking, no alcohol, no drugs and definitely no killing'

I'd heard about silent meditation retreats through my yoga teacher. Vipassana meditation is the practice of shared silence for days, sometimes weeks. When I heard about the retreat in Norfolk, I immediately signed up. Perhaps it was because the retreat ran over Christmas. Ten days away from all the madness. Not only that, Norfolk was not far to travel to over the festive season (although I did think it rather strange that such an 'exotic' retreat could be found in sleepy old Norfolk). Once I had put my name down, I didn't think too much about it until the time came to tell Dad I wouldn't be home for Christmas.

He sent a Christmas card, which arrived just before my departure.

Christmas without wee Kay, I can't believe it.

I hadn't done a lot of homework on where I was going, so it was a bit of a surprise when the taxi from Sheringham station drove away from the pretty seaside coast and up the steep hill behind the town, towards thickly forested terrain.

No sea air then, that's a shame.

Off the main road, the taxi followed a dirt track and emerged in a clearing. There stood The Vipassana Meditation Centre. Not quite what I was expecting. It looked like an outdoor adventure centre for kids, which, unfortunately, was exactly what it was. A big log-cabin style dwelling (hut) stood in the centre of a series of outhouses of various shapes and sizes and a grassy field.

'There's over twenty-five acres of forest around the centre,' said the taxi driver proudly.

'Sounds lovely,' I replied. 'Lots of places to go walking if the weather's not too bad.'

He said it was used year-round for group activities and adventure courses, but thankfully he didn't ask what I was there for (perhaps he knew) and I didn't volunteer.

In the reception, I met some of the other people on the retreat. The all-women group looked friendly enough, laughing and joking loudly as girls do when they're all thrown together.

Apparently, we were free to wander about in the grounds provided we stayed, 'Within the confines of the area clearly marked,' said the Indian lady as she pointed vaguely outside while collecting up our valuables for safe keeping.

'Please hand over your jewellery, phones and money before you go to your room, please. Yes, even your rings.'

The leaflet she gave us to read stressed the ban on *bodily decorations, no sensual entertainment or luxurious beds.*

I was beginning to get the picture.

We smiled at each other. I was quite looking forward to this new experience. It would be novel, at least.

卌 卌

There were fifty of us. The men's retreat was down the road in a similar set of wooden outhouses. There was to be no contact between the two groups.

'My husband's down the road with his chum, but we're not allowed any contact for the next ten days,' said a lady in the queue to be signed in. 'God knows how he'll cope.'

They'd only read the rules after they had signed up and hadn't realised they were not going to be together over Christmas, and that they would be thrown out if they were caught trying to meet or make contact.

Later that evening in the 'orientation', we would learn that in addition to the ban on hanky-panky, there was to be no physical contact (between anyone), no drinking, no yoga, no jogging, no smoking, no alcohol, no drugs and definitely no killing.

That last ban worried me.

Had there been 'killing' in the past?

We were assigned a room number and a map of the centre so that we could find where we were sleeping.

I went to drop off my bag, glancing longingly at the green fields and forests beyond the roped-off area.

Once inside the room, there was a polite, if rather sudden and desperate dash for the lower bunk beds as we grasped the full reality of the situation (it had been a while since any of us had slept in a bunk bed).

The next ten days were to be spent in these tiny, overheated barracks with a residual whiff of bleach and muddy boots.

It was cold and dark outside.

At 6.30 p.m. we duly trooped along to the canteen for our vegetarian meal. The atmosphere was friendly but the collective nervousness was palpable. Lambs to the slaughter, what on earth had we signed up for?

The real silence was to commence after the orientation session. Once we had eaten, a strange hush fell over the group as we were shown into the 'Dhamma Hall'. The 'Dhamma,' or 'the truth taught by the Buddha', is revealed gradually through sustained and serious practice and, through the course of the next ten days, we'd be guided in our meditation and supported in our learning. The 'Noble Silence' was to be observed at all times, and would involve a complete silence of body (!), speech and mind. It was rather daunting trying to take in all the rules, the schedules, the food regime and imagining how we would cope. But they reassured us that we'd soon settle into the 'drill'.

〲〲 〲〲

The wake-up call was at 4 a.m. with a bell (followed by half an hour for all six women to get up, get washed in the one bathroom and be ready for action). Rubbing our eyes, we filed into the school hall for our first two-hour meditation session. At 6.30 a.m. would come freedom. We could have breakfast and a long break of an hour and a half until 8 a.m. (ahhhh, what a relief! Eat, get outside, walk, stretch, gentle moan – to oneself).

To make things more interesting during the next three-hour stint of non-stop meditation, you could choose where to continue your own meditation after the first hour in the hall – the two choices were: 1) more group meditation in the now very smelly hall, or 2) own room meditation – go back to your slightly less smelly room to lie and meditate on your bed.

We all chose our bunks, much more comfortable meditating lying down (and occasionally snoring too).

Hurrah!

Lunch was at 11 a.m. and time for some more fresh air.

The afternoon began at noon with something new – a 'rest' period – when, if needed, you could commune with the teacher about any major problems you were experiencing or ask questions about Vipassana and the process. After the first few days, no one bothered.

Might as well be outside pacing along the perimeter like zombies.

Apart from 'dinner', the rest of the time between 1 p.m. and 7 p.m. was spent in meditation. We were all beginning to wilt by now so when the teacher's 'discourse' in the hall finally came around at 8.15 p.m. – preparing us for the next stage in our meditation 'training' the next day, adding some new aspect to our awareness of the sensations in our body and the teachings of Satya Narayan Goenka, who was named as 'the foremost lay teacher of our time', we simply didn't have the will.

We were ready for bed, more than ready.

And I could see some of the people on their perches in front of me were drifting off, head falling over to one side and then suddenly snapping back up to continue listening.

By then, we couldn't care less about anything, not missing our favourite TV programmes (or family) at home, or dreaming about the fish and chip shop down the road in Sheringham. All we wanted was bed.

So 9.30 p.m., 'retire to your own room and lights out' time was very welcome.

Phew, what a day!

꠸꠸꠸ ꠸꠸꠸

As is so often the case with retreats, the best part of the day turned out to be the meals. We were ravenous. Hence all fifty girls showed up at the dining room on time each day: 6.30 a.m. was breakfast, 11 a.m. was lunch and then at 5 p.m. there was the equivalent of dinner, the last 'meal' of the day, consisting of two pieces of fruit. Thankfully, breakfast and lunch were a bit more substantial and consisted of good healthy vegetarian fare (as much as you could eat) of Indian curries with vegetables or beans, nuts, dried fruits, salads, rice, all washed down with herbal tea or water.

So, it wasn't in any way a holiday.

It was hard going.

With just under twelve hours of meditation each day, it came as a bit of a shock to the system. At night the single bunk beds were so narrow that you had to sleep like a soldier standing to attention so as not to fall out. In the mornings, we would try to be out of bed just a few moments before anyone else to avoid the inevitable queue for the single bathroom before trudging out into the freezing cold. It was straight into meditation. And if you missed any of the meals, there were no snacks to fall back on. Nothing to keep you going. In fact, there was almost nothing at all but the long stretches of sitting together in a darkened room with the leader facing us – an example to us all – grey-haired and serene, like one of those scary teachers at school who keeps everyone in order without doing a thing.

She was at ease sitting in one position, effortlessly, for hours.

Unlike us, her 'new pupils', who wriggled and fidgeted as we tried, in vain, to copy her pose – back upright, cross-legged, hands placed on our knees, eyes gently closed. Instead, we were continually changing position, being coughed over by those with colds, falling off our carefully constructed perches (up to six blankets around or under us, propping up our knees, our back or bottom trying desperately to find a position that we could hold) while our leader sat there, Buddha-like, unperturbed, not a twitch or a muscle adjustment in sight.

The vegetarian diet wasn't helping – clearly some were not used to vegetables in their diet. Worse still, we were supposed to be thinking about our bodies and what we had been taught right at the beginning of the course before the silent treatment began – concentrating on our blood circulation, the tiny 'inner workings' of our system – not the myriad of other unacceptable subjects that would invade our minds. It was difficult to clear out all the rubbish.

Otherwise we had an area of a few hundred yards roughly cordoned off, in which to roam outside. We paced around the perimeter, behind the trees and bushes, going backwards and forwards over the two-foot miniature Chinese bridge. We sat on the single wooden bench, we lay on the bench, we got up from the bench (someone would immediately take your place) or alternatively, we'd go down to the bottom of the garden area where, if I stood on my tiptoes, I could see the town, the sea and presumably civilisation in the distance.

We walked alone and avoided each other's gaze (as instructed) to limit communication of any kind. We paced. We marched. We strolled. We filed. We slowed down. We stared into the middle distance. We stood and gazed upwards. We looked at the sun (that single day when it came out for us). We studied the grass, the sky, the insects, the shoes and boots and trainers and slippers of others.

We did just about anything to stop ourselves from going mad.

I didn't complain. I just put up with everything. My mother's words sometimes echoed around in my head, 'Keep going. Don't let the buggers get you down'. Perhaps it was my Scottish Presbyterian background that taught me 'You're not in this world to enjoy yourself' and that I'd interpreted this as doggedly not giving up, however hard it was, putting on a brave face and not speaking out, maybe even finding some strange kind of pleasure in the hardship.

〰 〰

Christmas Day showed up in the middle of the week. I sat down to 'dinner' admiring my artful arrangements of fruit. By now I'd learned to take my time and eat more slowly. My carefully washed, sliced and diced apple sat alongside my 'flourish' of orange segments, fanned out across the plate. This was critical to the enjoyment of each day. I'd peel, chop and set things out neatly, ready to eat one piece at a time, with beautifully carved peel curled up on the side.

It didn't feel like Christmas but I didn't seem to mind any more. I began chewing slowly, enjoying every tiny taste sensation. I imagined the family tucking into the usual feast – without me.

It wasn't that bad.

Midway through the retreat I realised a few of the group appeared to have escaped. They had just disappeared (the weaker-willed or perhaps the meat eaters – we would never know). Those of us remaining, the hardy souls, were left to shuffle into (or silently fight over) the precious extra space in the dark, hot, flu-ridden meditation hall. That lunchtime, the usual routine began. No one looking at anyone else, quietly

moving around the dining room, picking up the various offer-
ings of food, the cutlery, pretending to wait patiently for the
toaster, the only sound being the slicing, the quiet munching,
the noises of metal on crockery and knives and forks being
washed in the basins of warm soapy water provided.

Suddenly Wolf Lady (I'd given her that name in my mind
because of the jumper she always wore with a black and
white husky howling in a bleak arctic scene) let out a terrible
shriek right there in the middle of the dining room.

It was a chilling cry, like a beast being slaughtered. No
one knew what to do – we weren't even supposed to look
at her.

Was it safe to be here? (I remembered the 'no killing' oath.)

After a brief and tense few moments of silence nothing
else happened. So strange.

People settled back down to eating, realising it must have
been a cry for help or some kind of protest against the night-
marish regime she had happily signed up for last summer,
just like the rest of us, when it had seemed like a fun way to
spend Christmas. Ha ha.

We had no idea of course, we couldn't ask, we couldn't
speak, just had to assume. We'd never know. And so the
darting glances, the sense of panic, the frozen gestures
gradually subsided and soon the cutlery noises started up
again. In a moment it was all but forgotten.

卌 卌

Day Seven.

By now we had become accustomed to leaving the meditation hall during the session to return to the bunk bed – what a relief not having to stay in that pose, in that stuffy hot atmosphere with the dreaded coughers, but to be able to lie down or sit with knees bent, back against the wall for support. I had probably been muttering silently to myself on the way back (it became the only way to survive).

It was 3 p.m., dark, damp, drizzly and cold. I opened the door and began to walk towards my bunk only to fall flat on my face as I tripped over one of the others sitting meditating (very helpfully) right inside the doorway.

Of course it was one of those moments where you wanted to burst out laughing together and share the silliness of it all (what on earth was she doing sitting there of all places?). But we couldn't. It was forbidden to communicate or speak or share or look at each other in any way. And so, we had to try to muffle our giggles, stifle our amusement and marvel in solitude at the stupidity of it all.

The final day rolled round. We picked up our things, which were laid out in reception, and suddenly realised we were free to talk. It was a very special silence in that moment – for some, like me, it wasn't long enough, for others, well, they just couldn't wait to start talking again.

The whooping, the congratulating, the laughing and the excited talking all started up again – as if the ten days had never happened.

I quietly thanked the Indian lady. It felt strange to be using my vocal chords again and they sounded a little rusty. I picked up my things and started off down the track towards the station, smiling and waving to others who honked their horns as they passed by en route home for New Year. On the train, pleased to find I didn't know anyone, I wanted to be by myself and prolong the special experience. I didn't feel like reliving it in words with anyone yet.

卌 卌

Back at home, sitting on the sofa, wondering if I felt like watching *Mad Men* or *House of Cards* and whether to order a takeaway, I began to realise how much good the retreat had done me.

Yes, I'd actually learned how to meditate. By focusing on the sensation of circulating blood and energy flowing around my body, I'd stopped panicking, something I'd been doing more and more in daily life. The retreat had made me see that things I had come to believe were disastrous were not.

I began to appreciate how my thinking had shifted.

Life was good.

13

'The idea behind affirmations is to
change your engrained belief systems,
and lose the negative ones that might
be holding you back'

I had never been a big reader. I had always found my escape elsewhere – in work, in music or adventurous holidays. My career had become my main aim and my reading was geared towards that, meaning I had no time for reading for pleasure. My ex-husband, however, had made up for my lack of interest. He had books stacked high in every room; bookshelves jammed full and piles building up on the floor. There were always papers from work on the office table. He read the newspapers religiously every day and collected books on a wide variety of subjects – travel, geography, geology, the space race, politics and politicians, cultures, creativity, TV, film, Formula 1 racing, business and investment. He never tired of discovering new ideas, new approaches to life, and always seemed to have a firm grasp of the real issues, which he often shared with me. He did all the research, all the reading for us, and I'd just ask questions if I wanted to know – he was my very own walking encyclopedia.

Then we separated.

All of a sudden, I found myself with the time and inclination to start reading books. Uplifting books, spiritual books,

books on alternative therapies, neuro-linguistic programming, cognitive behavioural therapy, books on healing your past, books on childhood, relationships and women's issues. I became more interested in philosophers and philosophies: *The Meditations of Marcus Aurelius*, The Dalai Lama's *The Art of Happiness*, *The Road Less Travelled*, *The Secret* (but of course), *Awareness*, *The Alchemist*, *The Bed of Procrustes*, *The Little Book of Buddhism* with its wonderful quotations.

I now read in bed for hours – I took a book with me on the Tube, in the bath. For a time I'd carry the books around with me, reading, then re-reading sections that struck a chord, underlining bits that I loved and wanted to remember. There were notes in the margins and comments at the top of the page where I'd fold down the top or bottom edge of a page in a tiny little triangle so that, when the books were finished, if I flicked through them later, there was a clear hierarchy of importance. A fold down was very important, a light underline denoted something I thought was well expressed and a box framing a paragraph was worthy of extra-special attention.

I liked books with scribbles – it meant they were 'lived in'. My ex-husband would have disapproved of my habit of disfiguring books. In the past I'd been chastised for folding down the corners. But he wasn't around to chastise me and, to me, they were practical tools to help my understanding of how to live.

I discovered the books of Louise Hay. These books opened my eyes to new possibilities in my approach to daily life.

Affirmations could potentially change the status quo and redirect my future through positive thinking. The idea of being able to disengage from the private prison I had built for myself was exciting.

At last, a way out.

At the weekends I would go to the original Tea Palace in Notting Hill Gate for long leisurely breakfasts – white linen tablecloths, polished cutlery, perfectly cooked poached eggs with mushroom or asparagus, buttermilk pancakes and fresh cream. There were speciality teas to choose from – each in large glass containers or tea caddies that lined the walls. I'd order lavender or rose petal tea and listen to the calming music as I read. The idea behind affirmations is to change your engrained belief systems, and lose the negative ones that might be holding you back. Certainly my upbringing had been cosseted, repressed even, and I was very aware of my Scottish Presbyterian background and its strong work ethic. But I could see I had also absorbed, and accepted, certain family attitudes that perhaps weren't helpful; my experience of being 'seen and not heard' was hard to overcome. By developing a new set of beliefs and repeating them over and over as a routine daily exercise, you could breathe life into new ways of thinking, so that, over time, fresh positive beliefs would emerge and become established. It could give you greater confidence and a renewed purpose in life. Self-determination through a very simple process and creating a new you. It sounded good to me. After reading the book, I bought the audio version to play in the car – just to make sure I understood the approach fully before I started.

I also discovered Fiona Harrold's wonderful books on coaching yourself – even more work to be done on developing positive thoughts and changing negative behaviours. Once I had absorbed the key points, I began to test them out. First, I had to put together my list of affirmations – I didn't want to take on Fiona Harrold's or Louise Hay's suggestions exactly but had to admit they seemed good and would work for anyone, so I adapted a few for my first set...

I deserve to have more fun
I deserve to have more laughter
I deserve to have more money
I deserve to have more success
I deserve the very best and I accept it now.

Then I added some new ones of my own about becoming fitter and healthier:

I'm fitter and fitter every day
I'm healthier and slimmer every day
I'm younger and younger every day
I'm fit, healthy, slim and young!
I'm fit, healthy, slim and young.
I'm fit, healthy, slim and young.

It was all a bit far-fetched (younger and younger every day). However, I wanted to give it a try and didn't want to come across as old, grumpy and negative (although that's what I often felt like). If I hammered home youthfulness and cheerfulness, surely this would give me new impetus.

I noticed a change straight away.

People began making comments – 'You look great', or 'You're looking really well these days, Kay. Something good must be happening.'

'What's going on?' a colleague at work asked. 'New man?'

As instructed, I woke up each morning and looked directly at myself in the mirror.

This is a new day, a new me
I think differently
I speak differently
I act differently
Others treat me differently.
My new world is a reflection of my new thinking.

I began to wear slimline dresses from L.K.Bennett or neat pencil skirts from Jigsaw with tighter-fitting tops. I liked the new fashionable pointed toe boots even though it really wasn't the old Kay. For years I had sported neat, short haircuts and business-like trouser suits, spacious jackets and trousers with wide legs to hide my bumps. But now I grew my hair and had it blow-dried with a curl to match my more feminine look. Some colleagues gave me compliments in meetings, others just looked uncomfortable.

What was going on?

I put together a set of affirmations about work, about having better, healthier relationships and an exciting future – these were more elusive. Maybe they took longer? I saw no immediate change but I kept at it.

As I walked to work, I'd repeat the phrases to myself – thirty minutes of positive affirmations before I even arrived at work. Then by chance one morning I switched on Capital Breakfast. Until now, the only morning radio station I had listened to regularly was the *Today* programme on BBC Radio 4, which my husband never missed and I had worked on years before. But now I discovered that some people actually enjoyed a more positive start to the day. Rather than gloom and doom, wars and economic misery, some people cracked jokes; they were having fun. I loved Johnny Vaughan's sense of humour. He would always make me laugh with his 'Van Weasel' jokes. So maybe the 'I deserve to have more fun' affirmation had started working too? I couldn't remember laughing out loud on the way to work before, but now I did. Before Louise Hay, I would rarely arrive with anything other than a serious, anxious work-focused face.

And so things began to change.

I was thinner, a lot thinner.

At one point you could see my ribs; my cheeks were more defined (sunken), and I didn't look bad compared to the old chubby me. Even my boobs were more manageable and I happily pushed them into uplift bras to reveal, underneath, my new six-pack with 'dimples' in all the right places. I ditched the big black T-shirt and full-length yoga pants and wore brightly coloured cropped tops and short figure-hugging leggings. I was more energetic.

'If it grows, ead id. If it doesn't grow, douwn-ead id,' Louise Hay said in that lovely American drawl of hers (I used to mimic it when I repeated the phrases to myself).

I always chuckled at the American pronunciation of ''erbs' (herbs). And these food affirmations seemed to work for me too as I noticed I was eating more and more fruit and vegetables, more salad and soya-based foods, less meat and of course more ''erbs'.

Now in the gym, instead of doing my usual slogging away, breathing and sighing loudly during the laborious repetitive actions (endless arms up, arms down in time to the music, squat, squat, squat fifty times to strengthen the 'glutes', a hundred pilates hand flaps to tighten up the abs), I'd be concentrating on the affirmations and I wouldn't even notice the strenuous effort involved. Time flew by. My teacher called me the 'jumping bean'.

I'd chuckle when 'I deserve to have more success' turned into 'I deserve to have more sex'. Not sure where that came from but people certainly seemed interested in me.

It was working.

Then I'd have periods where I lapsed and nothing seemed to be going well again. Yet every time I lost confidence in myself or felt I had taken a backward step, I would pick myself up and start again.

Some of my affirmations simply didn't work.

Why not?

Was it because I was naturally impatient and didn't give them enough time?

Or perhaps they were too far-fetched and unrealistic?

Maybe it was simply because I didn't genuinely believe in myself or in what I was doing (I always felt uncomfortable in front of the mirror each morning, as Louise Hay recommended, talking to myself about how great things were going to be).

Money was still a problem – lots outgoing, nothing regular coming in. My redundancy money was dwindling fast and I'd soon be eating into my savings as replacement work projects were only sporadic at best.

And 'success' seemed to be out of my grasp, miles off in the distance and getting further and further away with each month that passed – for a time I felt I was moving backwards after the redundancy. But still, it was fun seeing how some affirmations were starting to take hold.

One evening, surfing on my laptop, I found courses in 'neuro-linguistic programming', which could take my affirmations on to a new level. I immediately signed up for an NLP retreat with someone who had used the techniques for years and experienced their amazing results first-hand.

14

'I had been doggedly working away on my affirmations to do with health, work and career, but I hadn't really thought about my love life. Here was my chance'

Florence was an experienced professional who worked with big business and was now running her own coaching consultancy. She had turned her attention to non-corporate clients like me who were looking to reset their life in some way. Florence was immersed in Neuro-Linguistic Programming (NLP), its potential, benefits and (almost guaranteed) success. There was a carefully worked-out method and if you were diligent in following the rules then you were likely to achieve whatever you wanted in life – true love, career success, great wealth, adventure, even living on your own desert island – anything was possible.

A chic redhead, Florence's experience in psychometric testing, leadership, team building, emotional intelligence, resilience and training were put to good use in establishing her distinctive NLP. Simply put, you describe what you want and then develop a set of goals and targets to deliver. Florence, it turned out, had plenty of challenges of her own. But, as the course came to an end, I was happy to sign up for another, so our friendship cemented and I came to know her well enough to understand her story.

This particular session took place on a Saturday in a pretty pavilion on the edge of parkland on the outskirts of London. There were six of us in the group. We were strangers. After tea and coffee, we introduced ourselves. Florence stood up at her flipchart at the front of the room and began.

'Today you can start afresh. All it takes is commitment, clear thinking and abiding by a few rules to keep you on the right track. You can make this the start of a new "you" and I can help you follow a process to guide you to your goals.'

Florence gave each of us a notebook in which to record our thoughts. The notebooks were covered in embroidered Chinese silk with birds and flowers in bright colours. Each had a long ribbon bookmark with an ornament at the end. These weren't to be thrown away after the session, but were to be treasured. First, we needed to shape our thoughts. Florence was providing a safe space in which to do this important 'work' and we'd have a trusted, experienced 'friend' to guide us through. And at the end of the day we'd have a blueprint for our future that we could take home.

We were given a few minutes to prepare our wish lists. It was a brainstorm in absurdity; when I read mine back to myself, I forced myself to ignore my doubts as Florence had advised us not to hold back, to be ambitious in our thinking and conjure up our ideal new life. We then had to review the list on a number of different levels.

Is the goal realistic?

Is it positive?

Does it affect anyone adversely? (If it does, scratch it out – your desires shouldn't hurt anyone else.)

What are the timescales you wish to set against the goals?

We spent quite a bit of time on this part of the session, as it was tricky translating dreams into practical realities.

IHT IHT

During the day, as a rest from the hard work, Florence described approaches that could help embed your new ideas within your psyche. She talked about creating a vision board. Florence kept hers on the fridge door. Someone else already had a corkboard hanging on the wall with various words, statements, images and objects pinned to it and they took the trouble to refer to it at least once a day.

It was important to be in a positive frame of mind when you looked at the montage and concentrated on the 'world' it created in order to imagine it into being. Other ways of imagining the future included affirmations. Having already had some success with Louise Hay, I felt mildly confident. I had been doggedly working away on my affirmations to do with health, work and career, but I hadn't really thought about my love life. Here was my chance.

Florence had brought a great pile of magazines and adverts for us to look at. We looked for inspirational images or scenes that were relevant to our 'dreams', cut them out and put them in our notebooks. We had to be as specific and detailed as possible.

I imagined the type of man I wanted to 'bring into my life'.

He was tall, over six foot, with black hair; he had to be 'well-built' with broad shoulders, a hairy chest, and large eyes – poor soul, it would be a lot to ask of anyone – but I continued with my shopping list. He had to have an interesting career, be an expert in his field and deeply involved in his work (just like me) and of course he had to love me completely. He would not have anyone else in his life (I knew where that came from) and absolutely no baggage from any past relationships. He would be smart and funny, younger would be nice and happy doing things that I enjoyed (another long paragraph, some unrepeatable here). The list reflected things that I had experienced in the past as having either loved or hated and I was trying to make sure that I eradicated the bad and highlighted the good.

Was it plausible to expect all of these things in one man?

Who knew?

We weren't to judge, just put down what we wanted and keep concentrating in order to make it happen.

卌 卌

It was a worthwhile day and we all left with our future plans mapped out in our notebooks. Over the next few months, I'd occasionally refer to it but, as it happened, my life didn't change dramatically. Eventually I shoved the notebook into a drawer, not disappointed exactly but perhaps a little chastened, and moved on to my next adventure. It would be another two years before I rediscovered it while packing up to move flats (yet again). Flicking through it, I stopped at the back where I'd written my list of character traits under *Ideal partner*.

And there he was.

My new partner.

As I began to read through the list I could scarcely believe what I'd wished for: the stage he was at in life, his attitude to work, everything fitted. In fact, I could tick off virtually every single characteristic on the list – well, all but one.

The physical description was very close, my new man was everything I could have wanted – and more – well, actually quite a bit more as he was a very big chap, tubby even. I wondered where that fitted in until I noticed on my list 'well-built' and another, underlined, 'must be well rounded'.

He was certainly that.

15

'The retreat brought out the best and the worst in people (as retreats often do) — introspection, judgement, tears, trauma, self-criticism, but at least everyone had time and freedom from their usual routine'

It was at another of these NLP residential courses in the countryside with Florence that I met Nadia. We three became close and Florence suggested signing up for a yoga retreat in a beautiful converted farmhouse in Italy.

Why not?

And so it was that some months later, we arrived at a secluded spot nestled high upon a hillside with its own pool and views across to the other side of the valley. The retreat was not far from Urbino, in Italy's Le Marche region that stretches from the Apennine Mountains to the Adriatic Sea. We were all a bit frazzled, having been in the car for hours, driving on the wrong side of the road with only a Sat Nav to guide us, bleating away its useless instructions in a thick Australian accent as we searched for a place called 'The Hill that Breathes'.

I'd found myself as the designated driver (Note to self: remember to stop chums having copious G&T's plus wine and port with their cheese on the plane out so that you're not left doing all the driving).

A few hours later, to our collective relief, we saw a sign for the farmhouse complex and abruptly, perhaps rather violently (the turn suddenly loomed up out of the blue), we veered off, tyres screeching, into a long, tree-lined dirt road.

We heaved a sigh of relief as we gathered up our things and congratulated ourselves on getting there safely, although we'd probably missed dinner and the scramble for the best rooms.

Ah, what bliss it turned out to be – our so-called 'F**k It' week or, as the children of the owners, two bright little Italian boys having the time of their lives, shouted out 'Fawk Eeeet'.

Initially, this was quite a shock to us.

Where was the yoga master, the quiet meditation room and the serene yoga types?

And who had permitted the use of such disgraceful language?

It turned out the owners of the retreat were ex-advertising people from London. They had decided to opt out, change their lives, dump the Big Smoke and run off to live up a hill in Italy, setting up a retreat for busy business people wanting to get away from it all. The couple had used their skills to produce an ad for the retreat starring their own two boys, who were filmed lounging about by the pool in their trunks, super relaxed. They were shot in the dazzling bright sunshine wearing dark oversized sunglasses, water glistening in the pool. One of the kids was lounging about on his big red lilo, arms folded loosely behind his head. He rolled over towards the camera and began to speak, in a wonderfully exaggerated Italian accent...

If yo tied of laif
If yo ad enoff
Yo dough need warree
Just say fawk eeet
An' every sing be aw-raeet

The retreat had everything you could possibly wish for – meditation, treatments in the tepees, fresh air, great food, Italian cooking classes, private pool, walks, views, trips to picturesque Italian villages with gelato cafes, romantic evenings by candlelight, informal talks about the owners' 'fuck it philosophy' and yes, even some yoga. There were over twenty people of all ages, mainly thirties and forties. We'd all gather together in the morning in the enormous Eden-style 'dome' for the first session of the day with the group leader John, who led guided meditations and explained his theories and helped us break out of our narrow thinking, our tendency to stick with things as they were, even things we didn't like, believing we couldn't change them.

He trounced all that. The retreat brought out the best and the worst in people (as retreats often do) – introspection, judgement, tears, trauma, self-criticism, but at least everyone had time and freedom from their usual routine. It had a profound effect on some people, others felt subtle changes, but everyone enjoyed the experience, whatever they got out of the week.

At night after dinner, I would sit with Florence and Nadia in their lovely room chatting about our lives, relationships, sex, books we were reading, discussing our fellow 'fucketeers' and what we were getting out of the 'F**k It' experience. I had my own lovely room, a necessary escape at bedtime – a chance to go through my own thoughts, make notes and write about the day's activities and how funny people are when all thrown together to contemplate their lives.

The couple who ran the retreat, John and his Italian wife Gaia, were very different personalities. He was mainly in the spotlight – he led the guided meditations, the breathing sessions, helped anyone who sought his advice and was generally the focus of attention each night over dinner. She was equally interesting: a fiery Italian, open and direct. Although warm-hearted, she would always say exactly what she thought without a care for its effect – a living, breathing example of the 'F**k It' attitude to life, long before they'd coined the phrase. We were told her blunt comments would occasionally cause uproar within the family.

'Poushhshhshshshshsh!' her husband exclaimed, exploding his hands up into the air to demonstrate their bomb-like effect.

We girls loved it: a strong woman who said it like it was.

There were more men than usual at this retreat – more than the token man I'd come to expect. I even bought the 'F**k It' book to add to my collection. It covers everything you need to know about the approach, has cute illustrations (another Gaia talent), lots of humour and techniques and tips for relaxing into the 'F**k It' way of life. It was liberating to be able to shuffle off life's worries – at least for a week – and to tell yourself to do what you want and if there's something you don't like in your life, then simply stop doing it and see what happens. Things won't fall apart and it might just help you find a new path.

16

'I learned a great deal from the group
and found the act of writing to be
therapeutic as well as creative'

As usual, I left the 'F**k It' retreat with a new friend, in this case a wonderful pilates teacher called Suse. After we got back to the UK, she began coming down to London from Lincolnshire for the odd break. A year or so later she convinced me to go on a writing course with her – she loved Mavis Cheek's style of writing and had found a week-long course in Snowdonia in Wales.

I was always up for new experiences.

This time, I found myself in amongst a group of enthusiastic writers, ten women and, yup, the one token man (again!). The majority of them had been writing for years. Some had already written novels or were in the middle of new works. Suse, already motivated to start writing, was excited by the idea of learning more about the craft and honing her skills.

I, on the other hand, had never written a single word, apart from producing written documents and presentations for work. However, here was the impetus to start as we had homework to prepare in advance. I wrote twelve short stories and a few poems in the weeks running up to the summer stay. It was a surprise to me that once I started writing I didn't want to stop. There seemed to be so much to share and so little time to do it all justice. It felt good. A friend emailed to ask if I was getting excited.

I wouldn't say excited, more apprehensive. It's supposed to be a holiday but I think it might be hard work and I'm worried about some of my writing – I know I'm supposed to be making things up but that all seems a bit flat – I need to talk about real life and things that happened to me. My stories are close to the bone and it's quite sad at times. I'm sure everyone else's work will be really inventive, clever and polished, so no idea how I'll get on.

It was a week of long days (and for me nights!) of intensive writing and trying out writing exercises in different styles. Then came sessions when we had to read our work aloud to the others. There was also plenty of time to get to know the group; we went on walks, took short trips to the local town and ate together in the beautiful house with its refurbished outhouses (it was a Grade II listed building where PM David Lloyd George was a former resident – it had history, I liked that).

We mostly sat round a large wooden table in the enormous lounge as Mavis helped us build up our skills and understand the various writing styles and approaches that can help produce interesting work, full of light and shade. We did exercises in dialogue, characterisation and each day we'd examine pieces of writing that Mavis had selected for us to review; we'd produce short pieces of work to show that we could adapt to different styles.

As I got to know the others, I realised how our individual experiences had inspired our writing in so many different ways. People's lives meant that they had stories to tell. Some were drawn to fiction, others history or memoirs. For me it was all about my experiences and how they related to my time growing up.

On the final night everyone was to read out one of their 'works' to the group. We all dressed up for the occasion, had a dinner with plenty of wine and then proceeded to the lounge upstairs. We all gave our performances. There was applause and a special thank you for Mavis who set us all on our way.

I learned a great deal from the group and found the act of writing to be therapeutic as well as creative. I was able to appreciate what's important to me, to organise my thoughts and even put my issues and feelings into some perspective.

We all had one-to-one sessions with Mavis and after discussing my work we talked about the inspiration for my writing – my childhood and the feelings of inadequacy I felt as a girl, which sometimes people took advantage of.

Mavis simply said, 'I wouldn't worry about those other people, forget them, just look at what you have, Kay. Look at what you have to offer.'

It was an important moment as it encouraged me to be more positive. At least for a while anyway. It would be several years before I could return to writing again. By this time I had a subject and many more experiences on which to draw.

17

'You seem to find things to worry about that are not really there or not as bad as you think. We just need to try to see what's at the bottom of it all'

After seeing Anna, my very first psychotherapist, on and off for nearly eighteen months, she moved away. I missed her sessions but felt I should be able to manage on my own.

A few months later I visited my new doctor's surgery in Notting Hill Gate for a routine check-up. I'd asked to see a lady doctor and she turned out to be someone who went the extra mile for her patients; she was in her late fifties and seemed to understand me in a way I perhaps hadn't anticipated.

'So, how can I help today?' she said.

Perhaps she recognised the changes I was going through and why I was so upset. I was constantly tired, my energy was erratic and I was experiencing sudden mood swings. Sometimes I would be busy and happy, the next minute I would crash and feel depressed. As a result, I was anxious and waking up with panic attacks in the night. She said we would do some tests to see if the menopause was kicking in as these were typical symptoms and she also gave me a list of people I could go and talk to. There was a long waiting list for appointments and it would be some time before I could start so, in the meantime, she gave me a list of people who could see me immediately but didn't charge a huge fee.

Vanessa was an old hand. She lived in a flat by the Thames near Hammersmith and practised from her home. She showed me into her office. It had an old desk with leather inlay, packed with papers on top and a set of old oak drawers on either side of an ancient wooden chair that creaked as she sat down. I was invited to sit opposite on the 'divan', a long sofa bed with lots of cushions. Some were hand embroidered, others were made of fur or hand-knitted wool, one had a pink heart and LOVE written across it in large letters. The room was stuffed full with too much furniture and all kinds of clutter.

I could see the bright blue sky and clouds outside beyond the high windowsill packed with ornaments – little animals, tiny china cups and saucers and small metal trinkets.

Vanessa was warm and friendly with curly white hair and metal-rimmed glasses that reminded me of my grandma's – a good sign. After the formalities, she asked me why I was spending so much time alone.

'What about your friends,' she asked, 'and family?'

'I don't want to bother people any more. After our divorce, I lost contact with some friends but I still have a few that are close enough to share this with – and already have, the poor souls! I think I have leant on them enough.'

'Why did you lose contact after the divorce? I'm sure most people understand.'

'I sensed they would disapprove, there's certainly a bit of "dividing up" that goes on, and it happens quite naturally. I have held back from some of my old friends as they were probably closer to my ex-husband and he needs his friends too.'

'What about your family? Where are they in all this?'

'They have their own problems and I didn't even want to tell them about the divorce at first. Because they were up in Scotland it was possible to hide for a while. It's embarrassing after being together with someone for so long. It wouldn't make any sense to them. It was even a good six months before I admitted to my father that we were separated. One day I called him up for a chat and he said, "That's funny, Kay, I'm just off the phone to Jonathan," and then there was a long pause.'

So I had to own up.

I was in tears.

'It's not Jonathan's fault, Dad. I didn't want to worry you. I still don't really know why it's happened and I don't want people to know we're getting divorced, especially as there was no one else involved, no real reason that you could put your finger on to quickly explain it all away nicely, done, dusted, clear, understood. I just changed...'

Dad didn't understand, of course. (How could he? He was of a different generation, you didn't get divorced and the 'change of life' didn't exist.)

Poor Dad. He couldn't comfort me, miles away as he was, up in Scotland. And yet he ended the call by saying, 'I'm always here for you, Kay, you know that, whenever you need me.'

Vanessa was sympathetic.

'It's good that you have family support like that. But you're here and they're up there, you seem sociable, friendly, bubbly, it's obvious straight away: you must make friends easily. Are you getting out and meeting people?'

'I'm trying, but I'm a bit of a loner. As a couple, my husband and I were always socialising and making new friends (like most Scots). I put on lots of big social gatherings, parties and get-togethers, but it was mainly for my husband – I would have felt guilty if I didn't. I really just wanted to be alone with him, living a quiet life with occasional get-togethers with close family.'

Vanessa asked about my upbringing: 'Did you have lots of friends or just a few close ones?'

I told her about the time I was ten when we moved away from the bungalow where I grew up. We were now living in a semi-detached villa in the West end of Greenock. It seemed very grand. It was very grand – I told my new friends at the Ardgowan Primary School that I lived in a 'Mansion House' (actually it was a 'Manse' – a house provided for the church minister who lived there before we moved in, bless!).

Dad painted and wallpapered the entire house, room by room, all by himself – he was good that way. One day I came back from a shopping trip to Glasgow with Mum and ran into the front room – it was huge, especially to me, big high ceilings, large sash windows with wooden shutters at the side, intricate cornicing and a large carved wooden fireplace that dominated the room. There were old newspapers on the floor, no furniture, bare light bulbs, shocking bright light and the smell of paint and wallpaper paste from his pasting table filling the room. He was up a ladder in his overalls with a paintbrush in his hand when I burst in, excitedly twirling about and pointing my toes to show off my new patent leather shoes.

A few minutes later I reappeared with the fancy bright red patent leather shoes that Mum had also bought.

Mannequin parade!

I don't think they could really afford two pairs of shoes for this cheery little fair-haired girl in her Sunday best just back from the big city, but they were so beautiful, irresistible and they seemed to make me very happy. Mum had given in.

'Your father was obviously important to you, Kay. Your mum doesn't get much of a look-in – we should talk about that. But I want to come back to you and your friends first, what about your friends at school?'

I tried to think back. It would only be in secondary school that I began to settle down with some proper friends – Jane, Mary and Jean – and that was much later. In my first primary school I could only remember Brenda round the corner, Innes along the road at the farm and Cecilia up in the council estate, but we hadn't kept in touch after I moved into town. For the next year I was in a school down the road from our new house while my brother was in the school for clever people up the road in the opposite direction, Greenock Academy. He had received a scholarship to go to the private school but I had to wait and sit an exam the following year to try and get in so we were apart and in different schools for the moment.

Mum was working for the directors of one of the big shipyards in Port Glasgow and had arranged for me to go to Grandma's at lunchtimes. That way I didn't see chums or have school dinners with them. Instead I went to Gran's (Mum's mum) on the second floor of a tenement 'close' (as we say in Scotland) in Roxburgh Street, which was half a mile or so from my school.

I loved going there.

It meant Mum could stay at work rather than rushing back home to look after me. Later, she found a job nearby when Glenn and I were both finally in the same school and we would all come home for lunch together, but for now this was my routine and I loved my gran.

Vanessa smiled.

'It sounds wonderful, Kay – you were really loved and looked after. But in the way you describe some of it, you seem to see "being different" as negative, as if you were missing out. Tell me a bit about what you liked about your time back then – what were your happy memories?'

'Music,' I replied, 'definitely music.'

And 'The Greenock Arts Guild', which was only a few streets from our new house. The Arts Guild was an important part of my early life. I seemed to do everything there; it was the place all the children in the area went to on Saturday mornings to see films. I remember watching *One Million Years B.C.* (quite risqué for young kids in those days), an audience of over 300 screaming children, throwing things, screeching, laughing, high on Kia-Ora orange juice, pink shrimp sweets, Black Jacks and Wagon Wheels with their soft marshmallow centres and great crunchy biscuit discs covered in a thin layer of ultra-cheap chocolate. Delicious!

It was where I had ballet lessons, elocution lessons (Mum and Dad got tired of listening to my lazy accent, which I'd picked up at school and it wasn't up to scratch apparently) and where I later attended some rather dignified chamber music recitals and string ensembles sitting quietly beside my piano teacher listening to Mozart, Schubert, Grieg, Mahler. It was very proper. I also took all my piano, dancing and speech exams there in the formal practice rooms – enormous high ceilings (even higher than at home) with imposing doors and frosted glass to keep out the curious. It was also where I took part in the many local theatrical extravaganzas including the annual ballet shows and the somewhat riotous school operas.

After all the fun of Saturdays, Sundays by contrast filled me with dread. While Mum made breakfast downstairs, Dad asked my brother and me some difficult general knowledge questions. We were in Mum and Dad's big bedroom, all bunched up together on the bed with the dog at the end.

'Kay, what's the capital of Australia?'

'Sidmouth?'

I invariably got the answer wrong. They laughed and poked fun until I cried.

Vanessa cut in.

'Do you think it would be helpful to try to see things differently, glass half full rather than glass half empty, Kay? I'm sure it wasn't that bad. Your dad probably just wanted to encourage you. It sounded like fun, all cuddled up in bed like that.'

I had to agree.

But the strange thing was it didn't feel like that at the time. I remember wanting the earth to swallow me up. I remember deciding there and then that I had to be clever – that's what seemed to matter – I had to outsmart them all – maybe I could be good at other things and show them I wasn't a waste of space. I was two years younger than my brother and he was special: he was well read, had a lovely gentle personality, was a natural student and liked by everyone. Actually, he was adored by everyone; he had even won the Best Baby competition at Largs when he was tiny and had a lovely little silver trophy to prove it so the accolades began early for him – teacher's pet. I sulked in silence. To make matters worse, I absolutely loved him. I looked up to him and admired his easy path in life. If only I could be more like him.

'You seem to find things to worry about that are not really there or not as bad as you think. We just need to try to see what's at the bottom of it all. And those panic attacks you describe, waking up in the middle of the night, terrified, I'm sure we can help you with those.'

At the end of the session, Vanessa handed me a tiny oval box.

'Take this and see if it works for you,' she said. 'Place the little figures inside under your pillow at night – many of my clients find it helps to take away anxieties and improves sleep.'

The object was shaped like a miniature Shaker-style box. It fitted neatly into my palm and was made of balsa wood, light as a feather. Roughly hand-painted on the outside, it had two red and yellow hand-drawn stripes. You opened it by removing the lid to find six tiny figures, all slightly different sizes, made of two matchsticks bound together like a cross and using brightly coloured wools wound around them – purple and red, black and gold, yellow and green, blue and orange. They had dots for eyes and smiling mouths.

There was a description of the group on a rolled-up piece of paper, which I uncurled, *Guatemalan worry people*, and instructions on how to use them. This was the sort of thing I always thought was a bit loopy but it was kind of her to give me the gift so I thanked her, popped the box in my bag and walked home along the river. I added it to the little collection of crystals and trinkets I was fast acquiring.

With all that positive energy around me, night and day, how could I fail?

18

'I was very inexperienced and insecure, physically uptight and embarrassed at the changes I saw in my body as I began to develop into a woman'

The Guatemalan worry people were clearly not doing their job. I was a nervous wreck. Without the structure of work, there was only me in a vacuum. I felt my spirits drop each time I arrived back at the flat.

I arranged another session with Vanessa.

I was still fretting and lying awake at 4 a.m., thrashing about, going over my life choices, my mistakes, worrying about people I had let down.

Back in her room, on the couch by the window, I'd just started talking when we were interrupted by a text message. Vanessa could tell I wanted to check who it was from. Even though it was over, I still wondered if it might be 'him' – Mr Egypt. I had taken to calling him Mr Egypt, not just because that's where he worked, but also because I was making a real effort to distance myself from him and the memory.

Instead, it was from an extremely distinguished and helpful Lord interested in the work I was doing in relation to the Olympics legacy. I had taken to calling him Lord 'Shower' after one particular incident. Vanessa wanted to know more.

To explain properly, I needed to go back to my own coming of age to give some context to what had happened outside the House of Lords one beautiful summer evening.

I had always been sheltered as a child. I'd missed out on those wild teenage years. I was very inexperienced and insecure, physically uptight and embarrassed at the changes I saw in my body as I began to develop into a woman. I put up with what my body threw at me and hid it away as best I could.

One day I found myself escorted into the kitchen by my father while the rest of the family was left watching TV in the front room. I sensed calamity; my father was the one person I longed to spend more time with, to be close to and respected by. But, as we sat down, I spotted a yellow and white booklet lying on the table with black writing and realised it was time for 'that talk'. I was mortified as Dad started to go through facts from the book: who does what, where it goes, what happens next.

'So, if you look at this diagram, then look at the picture of that part, you'll see the physical changes that occur...'

I sat there in tortured silence, blocking it all out as best I could. I might as well have had my fingers stuck in my ears. I didn't want to hear a word. My face was bright red. Looking back, I imagine it was also difficult for my father, but I'm sure he relayed the facts in typical male fashion – solid, without emotion; there you go, job done!

Next problem?

They say that by the time you are told about the facts of life you already know it all from school, but for some reason I had missed out on all of that. Perhaps it was because I had been at three different schools, and spent so much time with Gran at lunchtimes and after school, instead of with friends. I certainly hadn't been told anything at school. As a result it was all a most terrible shock!

Of course they did their best.

Of course I now see that my parents were doing what they thought was the right thing (this was the first time they'd ever had to do it, yes? and God knows what their own experiences had been like), but you don't think of that at the time. You think your parents are all-seeing, all-knowing and, perfect, just there for you.

My parents were very private people. They were uncomfortable about sex and nudity and how to deal with it. Their bedroom door was always closed (unless for the ghastly quiz times on Sunday mornings) and I never saw them naked. They were always dressed, in pyjamas at the very least, and behaved modestly. If something untoward appeared on the TV, Dad would exclaim, 'My, my!' and jump up from his chair to stride across the room to switch it off. If it was just some romantic stuff, he would say, '*Ah, la grande passion*' – and we'd all laugh, embarrassedly of course.

I tended to go for very nice boys, even though I found myself attracted to the bad boys in school (as everyone did). Later on in secondary, while most of my friends were out having fun and experimenting, I was seeking out sweet, kind, 'unpushy' types; 'nice boys' who wouldn't dare lay a hand on me.

I once fell for a lovely guy who I'd fancied for ages. We got together one night – a few modest kisses – and I was in clover. He said he would call to take me out. Little did I know that one of my friends had, behind my back, been in touch with him and they got together instead.

I cried and cried.

My best friend Jane was head girl. I adored her and looked up to her. She was pretty and very bright, good at hockey, always involved in everything and the centre of attention (especially with the boys). Mary lived just a few houses down from me on the same road. Mary was petite like me but a sweeter and gentler person you just couldn't imagine. She was always full of laughter, uncomplicated and easy to get close to.

After school, Mary and I would walk home together. The milk pan would go on the gas stove with full-cream milk before being poured into mugs or cups with freeze-dried Nescafé. We'd go upstairs to her room with the skylight windows and play records on the 45-rpm record player over and over. We loved 'Windmills of Your Mind', the theme tune to *The Thomas Crown Affair*. We talked about everything. Already I'd decided that I wanted to work for the BBC, she wanted to teach and sadly, Mary left school in the fifth year to go off to do teacher training.

Jane was a minister's daughter. Her house was always full of life because of all the church arrangements. There was a big Christmas tree, Easter services, watchnight services, Halloween parties and fun nights with the Youth Fellowship club in the church, which I joined to be with her. The best thing of all was the baking. Her mum was a great baker, presumably all the practice with the church events, coffee mornings and the Women's Guild meetings. On top of the high cupboard in Jane's kitchen was a huge stack of tins full of pink marshmallows and glacé cherry fridge cakes sprinkled with coconut, fruit scones, pikelets and chocolate crispy cakes. I tried to be good but I couldn't resist.

Jane preferred coming to my house, as my mum didn't have time for baking and all of our biscuits and cakes were shop-bought, which she loved.

So now I was a teenager and went from being a confident, cheery child, running about, arms open to the world to being an inward-looking young girl. I was worried what people thought of me and developed a tough exterior, a hard shell as my mum would say later (but with a soft centre). I began to build my protective armour and gather my arsenal of weapons to fight off the enemy.

What I lacked in social confidence, I made up for in my studies: I was a dedicated student. At university, when most people were out having fun and enjoying their freedom, falling in love or getting into trouble, I was in my room or in the library hard at work, even on the occasional Saturday night. I got up at the crack of dawn – I had arranged a special early breakfast at the halls of residence before any of the other students appeared – I walked twenty minutes to the music department and played the piano and bassoon for two hours before lessons even began.

What I failed to do was fumble around in messy relationships, the type that stand you in good stead for the rough and tumble of later life when you're figuring out who's good for you. Instead, my life was about getting on and forging a career.

When I had delivered – one MA Hons degree Music/French (including a lonely but successful year in Antibes in the South of France, where I worked hard learning to speak French), I moved on to my second degree (Bachelor of Music). In my final year I began to relax and found myself at student TV, getting ready for my next target – a great job.

Here, I met my future husband: handsome, kind, supportive, decent. He was smart and ticked all the boxes so off I went to London with my new partner and a career in the BBC firmly in my sights.

Jump ahead twenty years, my determination was as strong as ever.

I had become involved with what was to happen to the Olympic venues after the Games finished and, taking the lead, was the driving force in bringing on board companies that might be interested in being part of a new vision for the Olympic Park. Politics was an important element in framing the opportunity and with it, meeting politicians. Meetings were essential in promoting the initiative, some with smaller companies, but others with major business brands, and I soon discovered that several Lords were very supportive and keen to use their influence to help.

One Lord who seemed particularly helpful invited me to dinner at the House of Lords. He had asked me to wear something nice (I didn't think anything of it at the time, but how sexist!) and I made sure I was looking good, well turned out and appropriately dressed. A new, long and slim-fitting summer dress in brown with a neat belt, simple necklace and a light cream overcoat and silk scarf. I had a little tartan handbag with tan leather to match my shoes.

Over dinner we talked about the media legacy, what more could be done and who he could muster for the cause. I had one glass of wine (I don't really drink) and was too busy talking and getting excited about delivering on the vision we had been developing to notice anything odd. It was the perfect time for a new employment hub in London, right at the point where the digital world was coming together and organisations were beginning to change. The idea of East London married to such an opportunity for young people was compelling.

The next thing I knew he was telling me about a friend of his who had gone to a lot of trouble to give his wife a very unusual and special birthday present. In great detail, he described the birthday treat which had involved her being driven to a giant barn in the middle of nowhere, and there, a number of very handsome young men – hand-picked by her husband – were 'hers for the night'. Each of them would take her in turn. She was enraptured (apparently).

I had no idea how to react.

I laughed slightly nervously and changed the subject. After dinner, I was to be taken on a little tour of the House of Lords. By then I was used to having tea there, attending receptions on the terrace or formal parliamentary sessions so I wasn't sure what more there was to see, but this time I did see more, but it was the private rooms and quiet areas for study. Finally, he took me up a narrow winding staircase and into a small library. We stood there admiring the view, the books, the quiet, the stained-glass windows on to the Thames.

There was an uncomfortable pause.

'I must go, then, but thank you so much,' I volunteered, smiling.

Outside, as we parted, he came towards me and pulled me in for a hug and a kiss.

'I imagined you in the shower last night and you were very grateful,' he mumbled in my ear.

I stifled an embarrassed laugh and headed for the Tube as his text came in: *I enjoyed dinner so much. You're very, very special.*

Here, Vanessa stopped me.

'I think I get the picture. What does it mean to you, what do you think it tells you, Kay?'

'I need to get out more!' I said, laughing nervously. 'I'm so inexperienced that odd things happen to me and I don't have a clue how to deal with them. Suddenly living on my own, with more freedom – that's good, it's what I wanted – but I have to admit I'm also out of my depth. I don't want to be rude or ungrateful, I want people to like me and help me in my work, but I don't really understand what this is all about.'

'I'm afraid we have to finish here,' said Vanessa and asked me what I thought I should do.

I wasn't happy with these uncomfortable experiences; they wouldn't lead anywhere and yet I wished I could meet people who I wanted to form relationships with.

Vanessa smiled and encouraged me to take some practical steps to make this happen, to seek out new friends and make healthier connections.

19

I'd decided to start my search for new friends straight away and soon found myself booking a three-day singles break to Jersey. Well, why not? I'd never been there. Nothing drastic, but it made me feel better: I had a plan.

Our tour guide might as well have said, 'Are you *weirdos?*'

What he actually said was, 'Are you *solos?*' almost in a whisper, very slowly and with a creepier accent than Joe Grundy in *The Archers*. He said the phrase very quietly but deliberately, with the four syllables given equal weighting. 'Are – You – So – Los?' while leaning in to us too close – peering at us through his bottle-bottom glasses, piggy eyes staring out as if we were the creatures from the black lagoon.

I was in the middle of talking to my new friend Jenny whom I'd met the night before. We immediately stopped talking and glanced at each other, trying our hardest not to burst out laughing.

'Yes, we are,' we replied, giggling.

That probably convinced him we were good time girls.

𝍷𝍷 𝍷𝍷

I had arrived the previous night slightly later than the rest of the singles group on a Channel Islands flight in to Jersey and had made my way by taxi to the Pomme d'Or hotel. After I checked in and dropped my bags off in the room, I made my way down to the bar, where we were to meet. As I walked in, I was pleased to see a nice group already gathered – three guys in their late twenties, a couple of older men, well dressed, handsome in shirt and tie, accompanying two attractive women who were raucously laughing while holding large glasses of sparkling white wine in their beautifully mani-cured hands – bright red nail varnish with bright red lipstick to match. I was a bit nervous but approached cheerfully and asked if they were here for the three-day Jersey trip?

'No, dear, we're here with the funeral party. How about over there?' she said, pointing with one finger, still managing to hold onto the glass at the same time.

I turned round to see what appeared to be a church meeting in the corner, all in silence.

Oh dear – just my luck that the funeral party were having more fun than the singles, I thought, as I approached them, still smiling.

There were about twelve people in a semicircle, a real mixed bag of all shapes and sizes and a variety of ages, definitely some anxious, uncomfortable faces but thankfully, all with lots of glasses in front of them. I introduced myself and shook hands with everyone in turn. I sat in the free seat next to a girl called Jenny and we immediately started chatting about what we did and why we were there. Jenny was young, so out of place with the rest of us old biddies – most of us were aged between forty and seventy from what I could work out.

As usual, there were more women than men.

As usual, the women were more interesting than the men.

Jenny, in her twenties, clearly appreciated more traditional pastimes and wanted a nice holiday in good company.

Like me she'd thought, 'You never know, you might meet someone, so best to get out and see what comes along.'

We immediately hit it off, chuckling away at the ridiculousness of our situation, stuck in this very old-fashioned hotel in the middle of Jersey.

At dinner, as the wine flowed, we all got to know everyone, crammed together on a long, narrow table. Out came the stories, especially from the older men, who quickly took the spotlight, the life and soul of the dinner party. There were a few knowing glances between the ladies as they collectively clocked the cocky ones. Jenny and I chatted up the waiters, who seemed amused by our ensemble. We must have been a curious group – otherwise the place was filled with couples out for a romantic Saturday evening treat, enjoying the elegant surroundings with views across to the twinkling lights in the harbour.

What did we look like?

Wedding party? Wine club? Grandma's birthday night out? Saga business conference?

Some of us slipped away after coffee – a good night's sleep before the early start and full day of activities ahead. Others got busy and made the best of the bar until the wee small hours and, by morning, there was a new couple happily canoodling and holding hands like teenagers in the lobby. Geez, that was fast work!

So now, here we were, all gathered together in the hotel lobby at the crack of dawn for our first Jersey adventure – a 'walking tour' of Saint Helier with our local guide Archibald with the bottle-bottom glasses – taking in the sights, including Liberation Square, Elizabeth Castle, the floral gardens, the glass church, the beautiful beach and Nigel Mansell's fancy home (well, we stood outside his home and admired his enormous security gates).

Over the course of the next three days we all began to relax and enjoy ourselves. We travelled around the island, enjoyed the scenery, took buses, ate together or went off on our own then regrouped; we breathed in the fresh sea air. It was a lovely safe holiday for single people who don't always want to be alone. We spent time with different people in the group, came to understand our various reasons for being there and laughed a lot. Funny how first impressions are often misleading and, once you get to know people, you realise we're all just the same – full of doubts and insecurities, wanting to be liked, be appreciated and be part of something.

On the last day a few of us had lunch at a seaside cafe as the hot summer sun beat down and the sun umbrellas went up. It was a lovely end to the holiday despite the lack of trysts.

20

'The pill, smaller than an Aspirin, would be placed in a tiny brown envelope, folded over and sealed with its name written on the outside'

I had begun seeing a very experienced and recommended homeopath in Ealing – mainly for health reasons – but I soon found out that homeopathy was about far more than just physical ailments. I loved the way this ancient therapy treated the whole person, rather than focusing on a specific problem. After a few sessions I was hooked and began to look forward to my sessions with Laura – she was kind, thoughtful, under-standing and gave generously of her time and experience.

I'd arrive after the gym, tired and hot with another empty weekend ahead of me, a barrel-load of work to do and just feeling stuck. I thought I was done with Mr Egypt and was doing everything I could to move on, but the minute I started to talk and describe how I was feeling, I was in tears. Often I'd find myself in tears for the whole ninety minutes. It gave me headaches. Laura gently talked with me and sympathised. She'd ask me questions or tell me about similar experiences she had that might help me see that things were not that bad.

She knew about the menopause, the effect of the hormonal changes in the body for women my age – affecting moods, emotions and physical impulses – almost equivalent to the powerful hormonal changes you experience as a teenager. She believed menopausal symptoms were very similar as they were also caused by fluctuations in the sex hormones and that the menopause could even affect the way you think about sex and relationships. In some women, the effects of oestrogen and progesterone changes in the body can be quite severe. It seemed to fit with what I was going through – the impulsive behaviour, the mood swings, the depression.

She'd then begin flicking through an enormous homeopathic tome she kept on the desk beside her, presumably to find the perfect remedy for my symptoms.

Looking up, she'd declare, 'I think I know exactly what to give you today.'

Relief all round – a cure was in sight. Finally.

At the end of each session Laura would nip behind the door of the cupboard in her front room. I could hear her rummaging around as she opened and closed tiny little drawers then I'd hear paper rustling. Finally, I'd be told if she had this week's remedy 'in stock' or if I had to wait and have it sent to me by post. Laura took this part very seriously. She had just spent a long session listening to how I was feeling, and identifying the main cause of my deteriorating mental state. She was like a psychotherapist, listening, coaxing information out of me while sympathising with my plight. She'd note down physical symptoms as we went along. But now, she had to deliver the correct remedy to help nudge my system to heal itself and restore balance to my life.

The pill, smaller than an Aspirin, would be placed in a tiny brown envelope, folded over and sealed with its name written on the outside. I didn't like taking conventional medicines. I remembered Mum popping pills for her headaches – the downsides were never highlighted in those days, there were few warnings about adverse effects on the body and I think it led partly to her health issues later on – so I was wary. To me, homeopathy seemed a much gentler, more natural route to good health.

One day Laura gave me zirconium – an ornamental stone and an element formed over four billion years ago and used in the nuclear industry. She told me it was the oldest mineral on earth and yet one of the most commonly found minerals in the earth's crust.

Wow.

Laura and I had talked about new beginnings, being on the threshold of something big, being excited and fearful at the same time. It was then that she said, 'Ah, now I know what to give you today.'

Zirconium assists in starting something new, breaking with the old and making room for you to develop creatively; somehow it provides the push needed to get over any last-minute holding back. I anticipated nothing short of a seismic change. Surely my career would take off into the stratosphere. Or was it about relationships? Or the menopause?

I don't know whether or not, over time, there was a subtle and gradual improvement in my overall health and situation but I always felt better when I left Laura's – tension built up over the course of the week dissipated and she gave me confidence that what I was going through was normal. Weekly sessions kept me going for over three years and I came to trust her.

She often shared her own life experiences to provide alternative perspectives and told me that I should be kinder and more tolerant of myself. She encouraged a different view.

Even better, she provided me with a special secret weapon. It was always a tiny white pill, but each time a different 'prescription' appropriate to my situation at that precise moment in time. I would place the pill under my tongue either immediately or later before bed and let it gradually dissolve.

It would surely provide a magical solution.

21

I knew for a fact that the women paid the expensive joining fee because, being women, we discussed it. Women talk about everything after a couple of glasses of wine. We didn't ask the men if they'd paid but there was a nagging suspicion that some of them got in for free. They were old-timers who'd been 'members' for years, chums of the owners, possibly happy to be called up at the very last minute to make up the numbers and ensure that the ladies who had signed up and paid (there were always plenty of ladies) didn't outnumber the men.

'Dinosaur dates' as we came to call it must look as if it had plenty of eligible men on its books.

All the same, I was excited.

This was an exclusive club for a select group − not a huge network of countless pictures and profiles − and I had joined up with my friend Fran.

Fran was an expert. Over the years, she had tried lots of dating sites, agencies and organisations in the search for Mr Right. She knew how to get the best out of their events and special offers − and choice of men. She understood the pitfalls and how best to promote yourself and was, by now, so well versed in the various systems that she knew how to sort out the wheat from the chaff just by glancing at the men's activities and profiles. She had met quite a few and knew the ones who'd 'been around' on the website for ages. She could spot a dodgy one at fifty paces.

I was very grateful to have her as a friend, guiding me through the first steps. I didn't want to waste anyone's time, least of all my own. I'd made a hash of things in the past and realised I had to get myself in gear and try to lighten up. I was so impressed at how she always kept everything light and breezy, never too serious, and although she believed in the possibility of meeting Mr Right this way (and eventually she did!), she never came across as desperate.

What a pro.

By contrast I was slightly embarrassed and had no clue what to put on my profile – whatever I wrote, I came across as either too pushy or too silly. To make matters worse, I didn't believe I would ever meet someone this way. Fran realised it wasn't my type of thing after a few months – we went to some speed dating events together, where I always seemed to end up providing the guys with a quick counselling session rather than flirting. I couldn't help myself.

Fran then suggested joining an organisation that arranged special dates for small groups. It was more my kind of thing and she was happy to go along and try it out – another string to her bow wouldn't do any harm – she was on a roll.

When I looked through the schedule of events, it all looked perfectly lovely. There were evenings out in classy clubs, dinner and singing waiters and some amazing restaurants in London that I had never tried. There were options to visit stately homes, concerts, outings to Henley or Royal Ascot – definitely a cut above, we mused, as we discussed it in Fran's kitchen, presumably with selected gentlemen keen on meeting an interesting, professional, non-frivolous lady for a proper relationship. Hooray!

At the first event I could really see how the arrangement appealed to women like us, women of a certain age who had perhaps been single for a while, or divorced, widowed and looking for something better to do with what money they had, something sophisticated that could counter the disappointment of speed dating and dating websites.

This wasn't your drunken skimpy skirts and stiletto heels brigade – they'd have hated this. It wasn't just for fun. No, this was for more serious types, professionals who would enjoy meeting a variety of eligible partners in special places.

The seating arrangements were presumably organised to match up likely couples – lively personalities with the slightly quieter ones. At the singing waiters' dinner I found myself beside Roger, quiet but very pleasant, and talked happily in the brief time we had between courses and the musical interludes. The food was delicious and as we munched away, sopranos, tenors, ensembles and groups performed operatic arias, piano duos and lively Italian music from some of the best-known operettas. The singers also served the food, which was a nice touch. But I soon realised we'd run out of conversation. It was like having a meal with my grampa; interesting, but there was no spark or any possibility of romance. Fran seemed to be having a nice time on the next table. She looked beautiful – we had enjoyed getting dressed up in our cocktail dresses.

As I looked around, I spotted a smaller table with a lively group of eight – slightly younger, more attractive men and women who seemed to be having a raucous time together. It began to irritate me that we weren't encouraged to move around and meet a few more people rather than being stuck at the same table all night.

The day after the event, the owner called to see how I thought the evening had gone.

Did anyone take your fancy?

'If it's OK, I'd like to try the younger table next time, please,' I said.

'Oh!' She went quiet for a moment before continuing. 'Well, you see, Kay, from my experience men don't like to go out with women, the same age or older, they are all looking for younger women you know, that's just the way it is.'

What a cheek.

She went on, 'I specifically put you next to Roger as I thought you'd get on – I could see you were getting on like a house on fire and in fact Roger called me up this morning to say exactly that. He thought you were lovely and would like to see you again.'

I wanted to say, 'Oh, you mean the baldy guy with the tiny line of moustache who is about seventy and a grandad?'

But I didn't. Actually Roger had been good company, but was she serious about a match?

'Roger's a lovely man,' she said, 'I've known him a very long time.'

'He was very nice, a real gentleman, but I'm not interested in him that way,' I said.

'Oh, that's a pity, Kay,' she said with real feeling, slightly annoyed (perhaps she was on commission). 'He said he would absolutely love to take you out to dinner and have a proper chat, just the two of you. Are you sure you wouldn't fancy that? Why not give it a go?'

'I don't think so. I wouldn't want to imply I'm interested, so probably best not. Besides, I don't want to waste anyone's time.'

'No, I guess not. Ah well, I'll go back to him and let him know [I grimaced down the phone, hoping it wouldn't be embarrassing if I saw him at another "do"]. Maybe next time – are you coming with us to Henley? It's always fun and there's a little more mingling with everyone – we sail up and down in a fabulous vintage yacht – plenty of champagne – and finally stop at one of the beautiful country houses along the banks of the river. There's a silver service "luncheon" (!) with more champagne and you can walk round the grounds before setting off on the yacht back to dock.'

It all sounded lovely and I felt a bit guilty that I had turned Roger down. Amazing how so many of us women feel guilty about saying no – even if it's a definite no, when most guys wouldn't give it another thought.

Time to move on!

The best thing about dinosaur dates was that I met some fantastic women and we still keep in touch. We had such a good time, laughing not only at ourselves and our 'dates', but also at our predicament – looking for fun things to do and maybe even a man along the way; the groups were always full of strong women. To me they were all attractive, accomplished and able to look after themselves, financially and otherwise. You had to feel sorry for all those men in amongst this Amazonian tribe.

Although most of the men were nice, ultimately 'nice' wasn't good enough. Most of us agreed that we were probably not going to find Mr Right, but I certainly would recommend the experience. It gave me a chance to dress up and get out rather than watching TV on my own. It stopped me feeling unhappy.

22

'Out it poured, all the mess — my past, my childhood, relationships with men, endless hard work and sheer frustration with life'

Out of the blue I received a letter from my GP offering me an appointment with a psychotherapist at St Charles Hospital in Ladbroke Grove.

Each therapist brings a different perspective so I thought it was healthy to move on.

Vanessa had said to come back if ever I wanted to pick up again, but she, too, felt that I was stronger now.

I was very lucky to be offered some sessions with David.

I wondered if, as a man, he might be able to shed some light on the issues I was having in my love life.

And so, with great expectations – as always – I went along to see David for the first of six hour-long sessions in a tall narrow room at the back of the Victorian St Charles Hospital.

To get to the hospital I had to pass by the Carmelite Monastery in St Charles Square. I had seen a documentary about the nuns who lived there, and whose lives consisted of prayer, work and meditation. They maintained silence throughout most of the day and rarely set foot outside. There were hilarious scenes of a couple of nuns attacking an overgrown creeper in the grounds of the monastery, broad smiles, chainsaws in hand; another one of them cheerfully handwashing their linen in ancient metal sinks, and glorious choir singing.

After my disastrous adventures with men, I found myself wondering if the life of a nun might be for me.

Bliss, I thought, as I passed by the arch to the monastery.

But I bet it wasn't easy, cooped up in that cold, claustro-phobic-looking building with all those women making sacrifices, knowing that they were stuck there for the rest of their lives.

It was deathly silent.

David was tall and stooped with a nervous manner. I followed him into his room and sat down. There was a wooden table in the middle, a clock on the wall, a high arched window with security bars across it and frosted glass halfway up. There were a few black plastic chairs upholstered in bright blue material and a filing cabinet in one corner. David took a few minutes to tell me how things would work, how the sessions would run and gave me a form to fill in.

I looked down at the A4 sheet of paper. It had clearly been photocopied a zillion times – the letters were slightly fuzzy and the page was off-centre. At the top it said, 'On a scale from 1 to 10, how are you feeling today?' and then a list of questions including: 'Do you feel motivated, interested in doing things?' or 'Have you had feelings of depression, feeling down, feeling hopeless?'

'Do you have trouble falling asleep – too much, not at all, sometimes, most days, every day?'

I ticked the boxes.

Have you ever felt you would be better off dead?

Gosh.

Actually there were days when I felt suicidal, but it was rare and usually triggered by specific disappointments, leading me to dwell on the negative side of things.

I handed it back to David, who skimmed through the answers as he spoke, 'Keeping a diary of moods is important while you're seeing me. That way we can monitor how you are and can keep a record of how things are progressing, what changes are taking place.'

Finally, he looked up, 'What would you like to talk about today, Kay? What's going on in your life right now?'

I'd been composed, workman-like, filling in the form, but now – given the opportunity to share my feelings – I burst into tears.

Poor guy had no idea what had hit him.

Out it poured, all the mess – my past, my childhood, relationships with men, endless hard work and sheer frustration with life.

He looked as if he'd been blasted by a 100-mile-an-hour gale force wind but as I went on, he stopped moving about in his chair and started listening intently. Occasionally he would interrupt with a question:

'Do you know why you made this decision?'

Then off I'd go again.

'I don't understand why someone could treat me this way – are some men completely stupid and insensitive?' (I was back on 'him' again.)

The hour flew by. The box of paper hankies gradually emptied and my eyes felt red and sore with all the dabbing at my cheeks and blowing my nose.

Finally, with me still mid-flow, ranting and sobbing, David interrupted:

'Well, I'm sorry that we're now out of time today, Kay. Lots to do, I think.'

I stopped dead. I was so embarrassed, what was it all about and had that outburst helped?

The session was over.

I thanked him and left the building, empty, depleted. I had brain-dumped my life on David, poor soul.

At the first cafe I came to, I went in and ordered a cup of tea. As I finished it, I realised that I felt better, less gloomy.

卌 卌

The following week, I was back there again.

'So, tell me about the men in your life, Kay.'

'I never felt I had any say – right from a very young age, it was always the men who called the shots. They weren't around much but it was the men who made the decisions, had the power, held the purse strings and kept you "in your place" and, if they had to ignore you, it didn't matter, it was just the way it was.'

I had escaped this fate, running away to London, setting up home in another world where you had freedom, a chance to express yourself and grow, not just at work but at home, too. My ex was perfectly happy with me calling the shots; in fact, it often suited him. I liked to do the driving and he was fine about that – he preferred navigating. He did have to leave me for work in Hong Kong – I encouraged him, for his career – but it was nearly two lonely years without him. He came back as he knew it was better for us. He did have some things that were important to him and I learned from him – he always liked to do the right thing by people, he always 'paid full fare on the bus' – he was traditional and decent, he understood the value of being loyal to others and would never treat people badly. He behaved with kindness, not just towards friends and family but everyone, even in business. Sometimes it didn't pay off but he'd simply say 'as my father would always say, it's better to be done than to do'.

And yet here was Mr Egypt bringing it all back, the ill-treatment, the lack of concern, the marginalising. He wasn't there much, and just picked me up and dropped me whenever it suited him. I soon felt unimportant, like he could take me or leave me depending on his whim. I had no power. It was obviously easy for him to disappear when it suited.

It was then that I realised who Mr Egypt reminded me of – the male figures in my childhood. My grandfather, for example, he had no time for me, it was all about the boys. Then there was my father. I'd always longed for my father to be there, but he was away so much of the time and I had to wait my turn for his attention when he was home. He and Mum had catching up to do, they needed time together, time with their friends, their lively, smoky parties, elegant clothes, cocktails, Black Magic chocolates – wheeling in the trolley with the hot savouries and sandwiches with crusts carefully removed. I'd help Mum with the cheese cubes and pineapple triangles on cocktail sticks. It was fun. But there was little time with Dad.

What time he did have seemed to be reserved for my brother, or shared between us.

My brother was pushed and encouraged at school because he was a boy. But even my beloved brother could make me feel inadequate. I remember the panic, feeling vulnerable, as he climbed on top and tried to smother me with a pillow. I was going to die. I couldn't breathe.

Get off. Get off.

I could hear him laughing as he pinned me down and pushed the pillow over me again.

Mr Egypt, this distant figure who I had fallen for, dedicated to his work, often absent, was another version of the male figures in my childhood.

'Did your mother see it this way too? Did you discuss it?'

'No, never. I look back and think that Mum and I were, in some ways, both scrapping over the crumbs. We knew our places in the hierarchy and mine was at the bottom of the food chain. And in my experience, women don't really help each other out as much as they should, as much as they can. We might be "sisters" but there's some fundamental position that's hard to shake off whereby we're right back in the cave, all the women grouped together, tending the home, fighting over the small things in our confined, restricted world, and worse, fighting over the men and our position in the pecking order. It's quite astonishing how such things have persisted over millions of years without real change. We're back in the Stone Age. Anyway, that's how I feel with this man. It's raw, it's infuriating and I can't move on. I'm pinned down and being smothered by the pillow again.'

My six sessions with David were tough but we did uncover possible reasons for my anxiety that I would need to deal with in future. Six sessions weren't enough – but it's never enough, is it?

23

Shortly after my sessions with David ended, I received an email from a friend I had met on an Ayurvedic retreat. She told me about a 'miraculous' female psychologist she had been to see who had magically eliminated a toxic boyfriend from her life and recommended I go along for a try-out session down in Hampshire. Her name was Linda.

The journey to and from my fortnightly appointments took almost an hour and a half each way – a huge three-hour commitment for a one-hour session – but my time with Linda turned out to be rather special. And there was plenty of time for reflection en route. In fact, she was part of what I'd describe as a holistic wellness centre – a small team of professionals – clinicians, chiropractors, yoga teachers, nutritionists – who worked in an integrated way and all carefully managed by Linda to help people towards better health.

They tried to avoid the use of drugs where possible and talked in terms of vitamin deficiencies and nutrition; supplements were recommended to support my immune system. I saw the chiropractor when they suspected my skeletal structure was out of alignment. I even had a yoga class after my psychotherapy appointment – right there in the clinic. I tried most of what was on offer, including breathing exercises, guided meditations and hypnotherapy.

卌 卌

'Shut your eyes and describe what you feel.'

Linda had placed two small objects in the palms of my hands, one a soft toy, malleable and smooth, the other stiff and jagged.

I lay in a trance-like state and described the memories the objects triggered, some frightening, some joyous. She was strong on childhood as she was researching the subject in conjunction with a local university. She knew a lot about childhood adversity and its potential impact on adulthood. She liked the fact that I didn't hold back; I was honest and forthright and she constantly encouraged and reassured me along the way. She seemed to accept and understand why things were coming up now, late in life, particularly in relation to men.

'Start trusting yourself, Kay. Follow what makes you happy and push back on the things that don't feel right.'

She was able to use hypnosis techniques to get rid of unwanted thoughts and beliefs. The idea of being able to 'wash that man right out of my hair' was irresistible.

'Pouf, and he was gone!' my friend had said.

But, to my surprise, before we launched into any of this, there was some groundwork to do first. I hadn't hit the menopause yet but I was all over the place, mentally and physically, and she wanted to pull some facts together before treating me. A few weeks later, once I'd been tested and was now taking a variety of supplements to give me extra energy and sort out some deficiencies in my system, I asked Linda to remind me what each of the various pills and capsules were for so that I was absolutely clear on their purpose and benefits. I had been prescribed: magnesium, glyconutrient complex, vitamin B complex, core level adrenals, rutin, vitamin C, super digestive enzymes and high-strength omega-3. I told her I was also taking some evening primrose oil that I had bought. She emailed back straight away that evening.

Hi Kay, Answers below on food supplements, etc. Hope this helps. Lx

Magnesium – *continue to take until the night cramps subside, resume whenever cramps reappear.*
Glyconutrient complex – *this is a wellness supplement so continue as long as you can.*
Vitamin B complex – *this should be taken in the fifteen days leading up to every period.*
Core Level Adrenals – *continue until you have finished the full course.*

Rutin and Vitamin C 500mg – *take when you feel run down and lacking in energy.*

Super Digestive Enzymes – *take two with water before each meal (if you only eat twice a day, take four).*

Omega-3 Fish Oil – *a wellness supplement* – *take for as long as you can. I've given you something as a standby whilst I await the post (from the US, where stronger doses are available over the counter).*

Evening Primrose Oil – *not necessary if you are taking a good-quality omega-3.*

My time with Linda was productive and as much about general health and wellbeing as psychotherapy. I reaped the benefits almost immediately and began to feel better. When we eventually moved on to my personal issues for some reason I found I was less bothered about 'him', and after telling Linda the story – by now an old and well-trodden tale – she didn't seem that interested either.

She was far more interested in someone new that I'd mentioned in passing, someone who had turned up almost out of the blue, an old friend that I hadn't seen for years. And she also wanted to hear about the connection with my ex-husband who had joined me to help start up a new company. We were still friends and, now, work colleagues too. We'd started talking about the Olympics work early on because we were both interested and continued talking about it after I lost my job – he was keen to help make it happen. So, while it was all still a bit of a muddle, Linda observed what was making me happy and encouraged that.

It was about moving forward and looking for the positives.

I continued going to see her for nearly a year until the owner of the flat I was renting in Holland Park decided he needed to sell so I had to move on again. Since I was doing more work in East London, I'd decided to move to Canary Wharf. I sold my car (no more Hampshire) and moved into a tiny one-room studio with a view across to the high-rise buildings – a bit like New York, but a fraction of the size. I was happy there – it was like living in a hotel with a pool and gym and a bar up on the thirty-first floor. But it didn't take long before the tiny confines of my room with its pull-down bed, the cold and clinical environment of Canary Wharf and the distance from everything and everyone began to take its toll. So when I was to be unceremoniously turfed out only a year and a half into the tenancy to make way for a super high-paying, short-term renter just there for the Olympics, although inconvenient, it was probably a good thing.

I had to start making plans once again.

24

'When my yoga teacher in London suggested
I join her and some of her Indian friends on an
Ayurvedic retreat in Kerala, South India,
I wasn't going to say no'

I'd become pretty serious about yoga. I'd tried different types with different teachers in retreats ranging from Turkey to Italy, France, Spain, Greece and even the Isle of Wight. The women I joined on these retreats were studious and diligent, intent on improving their teaching methods, as well as their personal practice. The all-girl weekend yoga retreats that I joined took place in the tiny village of Nettlebed and were, in fact, full-on formal yoga training weekends for diploma students. The ten-hour days of yoga were more than a little advanced for me. They were strenuous and challenging, but I jogged along with it all and managed fine.

I learned a lot. I enjoyed the music, camaraderie, simple food and lodgings. It was healthy, not just physically (the diet was always home-made, simple, vegetarian) but mentally too. We would spend hours in the evenings after dinner talking and exploring alternative therapies and spiritual beliefs from different cultures. Animal cards and angel cards would come out, along with dousing paraphernalia. One of the yoga students was a trained astrologer who would later do my chart. These get-togethers really piqued my interest in other therapies.

When my yoga teacher in London suggested I join her and some of her Indian friends on an Ayurvedic retreat in Kerala, South India, I wasn't going to say no – I was on a journey and keen to go deeper into this world of spiritual wellbeing. And, where better to experience it, than in the country of its origin – India, amongst a friendly group of like-minded women.

I knew nothing about the Ayurvedic approach to health other than the majority of India's population use Ayurvedic medicine in their daily lives. It's one of the world's oldest medical 'systems'. It focuses on 'life' and 'knowledge' and the interconnectedness of people, their health and their environment. Ayurvedic doctors prescribe treatments for each person according to their own unique set of needs; it's holistic and specific to the individual. Their 'prescriptions' included food recommendations (diet), body treatments (massage), cleansing treatments (including total detox and 'purging' medicines), exercise programmes and lifestyle changes.

All sounded good to me.

Work had been going well at that time. After running several big client accounts single-handedly over the preceding year for the media company, I was handed a promotion and asked to recruit and lead a team of account handlers so that we could give our clients a better service. I had recruited three strong team members and they were beginning to demonstrate their worth, allowing me to feel relaxed about taking two weeks off work.

卌 卌

It was an idyllic spot with white sandy beaches and crashing waves. I breathed in the fresh sea air and looked up to the tops of the tall palm trees hundreds of feet above, sloping in the direction of the wind. A world away from London and a refreshing change.

The Ayurvedic day began very early – just before 6. a.m. – with the faint sound of an old handbell clanging in the distance. The bell became louder as the man with the bell toured the compound. Then came a firm rap on the wooden door to let you know it was time to get up. My cottage was in fact a mud hut: small and round, perfect for one. The overhanging roof provided shelter outside for the hammock. Inside, a noisy ceiling fan stirred the air above a large wooden bed concealed by a mosquito net neatly tucked in around the mattress – several scary holes clearly visible.

The compound was made up of a maze of huts of different shapes and sizes, connected by steps and winding terracotta tiled paths. Some of the other girls were sharing larger cottages but I was happy by myself and excited at the thought of all that lovely vegetarian food, yoga and healthy outdoor activities – paddling and swimming, not to mention the pampering, three hours every day.

The bell-ringer had gone. Silence now. Time to get up. I jumped to my feet and dived into the shower – dodging the mosquitos waiting for me. I was soon walking briskly towards the Ayurvedic 'hospital' in my towelling robe and sandals to report to 'Doctor'. The Ayurvedic clinic was a medical facility – starched white coats and clipboards. There were forms to fill out and nurses and private consultation rooms for each of us in turn. We all had an examination, a physical check-up and case history. We then had a one-to-one assessment with our doctor, who told us what to expect in the coming days. We were prescribed specific foods depending on our constitution – there were strict diets and a complete detox for others with more 'serious problems'.

I was disappointed not to have been diagnosed as a basket case with serious issues. I wasn't designated a particularly special diet, although, interestingly, I was to told to eat only foods that suited my 'dosha' or body energy. After the initial consultation, they took measurements – my pulse, height and weight – and looked very closely at the state of my tongue (!). Finally, I was told I was predominantly a 'vata' body type (the other body types are 'pitta' and 'kapha'). It seemed to fit – vatas tend to be always on the go, energetic, creative, lively and enthusiastic, with a lean body (when in a good, balanced state, I hasten to add!). Vatas love new experiences (that seemed to fit) and lots of excitement (yes, please); they are quick to fly into a rage (oh dear, I suppose so) but also to forgive (phew!). When out of balance, vatas worry a lot and suffer from poor sleep and can easily feel overwhelmed. When overly stressed, vata people often blame themselves (that's spot on, but don't most women blame themselves for everything?).

The doctors also prescribed a tailor-made programme of therapies based on their findings. Hooray! Every morning was to begin with three hours of massage with not one, but two therapists.

Turmeric. That was a surprise. The exfoliating was carried out using turmeric powder with extra grit added. The dark yellow powder was sprinkled all over one side of your body then rubbed deeply into the skin. It was then removed, gathered up and piled in neat mounds at the end of the hard wooden table just beyond my toes before the next 'round' would begin all over again. Both girls were brisk, professional and perfectly synchronised, using strong and even strokes, wide, circling movements all over my body in a pre-prescribed order. Obviously well trained. Then came the hot oil. The actual massage was different every day but was such bliss that even when the three hours were over, you wanted more!

Massage time was divided into three hour-long sessions, each with a different massage style or technique. There would be continuous herbal 'pumping' – muslin bags filled with fresh leaves or herbs and saturated with warm herbal oil applied across the whole body. Another massage involved lying on the ground on soft cushions and blankets while the therapist (holding onto a soft rope hanging from the ceiling for balance) used her feet to perform the body massage – a completely different experience from hand massage using gentler pressure of the sole. Another, perhaps for me the best massage, was with warm oil poured continuously onto your forehead in a slow, steady flow for an entire hour: it was called 'shirodhara', leaving you feeling very spaced out afterwards.

After the massage and a brief rest to recover came breakfast, a buffet of vegetarian food, fruit and vegetables, all dishes carefully marked out for the three 'dosha' types.

After a couple of days I'd got used to the drill – the early-morning massage followed by time to relax, beach, visits to religious shrines and temples or just sitting with chums under the palm trees, drinking fresh juice served in coconut shells. In the evenings there was a range of activities – music, theatre and astrology. There were Indian dancing displays, sitars, drumming and clapping.

Our group was made up of fifteen girls, including lawyers, media people, techies, mums and daughters (and one granddad – the token man).

The big treat was special sessions with the yoga master, who taught us new meditation techniques. One day we were given eye exercises to loosen up and tone the eye muscles. It had a real impact on my eyesight and, after the holiday, I no longer needed to wear reading glasses – miracle! It stayed that way for a long time and I was always grateful to him for demonstrating the power of yoga in this way.

The Indian astrologer had been an eminent doctor who had decided to leave his profession to become a full-time astrologer. Those of us who wanted to see him (most of us) had to provide our details ahead of time so that he could plot our birth alignments, look at what the future held in store and prepare a 'report'. Some people were very disappointed. They knew their date and place of birth but not the exact time, which meant that they could have a session but the results wouldn't be accurate; it's all based on the exact position of the planets at the moment you are born. I knew exactly when I was born – at exactly five minutes to midnight – it was recorded on my birth certificate.

Even with dropouts, by the time the astrologer came to us at the retreat, he had a full afternoon of sessions lined up. I was one of the last and impatient as usual. Eventually my turn came. He was sitting at a table with a few pieces of paper in front of him. Behind him was a view of the neatly trimmed lawns with a few clumps of two or three palm trees and a hammock, empty and still.

In his shirt and tie, despite the heat, he looked like a doctor, smart and professional. He beamed broadly as I entered. His English was perfect.

I wanted to know why he'd changed profession.

He told me his interest started from a young age. That while he had been encouraged to become a doctor, he'd always been interested in astrology and had continued his 'hobby' throughout his career until one day, he decided he was going to change direction and become a professional astrologer.

His astrological studies had been a revelation to him. He continued to discover new possibilities and began to see truth in the 'science' and, although some in the medical profession were dubious, he kept on. What was significant for him was that he saw what it could do for people.

༩༩ ༩༩

Over the years he had studied the history and philosophy of astrology, read everything he could lay his hands on, discovering that he had a talent in interpreting charts, which was the basis of readings. People responded to his interpretations and came back for more.

What an amazing story.

We began our session. I listened, nodding in agreement as I took notes. He offered insights into my career, personal life and relationships, and my health.

He said I was going to leave my job and have a change of career; that I would have many difficulties and false starts after my new beginning and I would explore many different avenues before I found the right thing for me.

I was excited when he said that the right thing would be something creative; that after spending most of my life working for other people, I was approaching the time when I could start to focus on myself. If I didn't, I would be unhappy and become ill.

I would become known for my hard work and perseverance; I would become successful eventually but this wouldn't happen until much later in life, and that I would have to wait. This would be difficult for me, but there was no way round it.

I laughed.

'That's the story of my life,' I told him. 'Impatient, held back, having to learn to wait. My most difficult challenge.'

He told me, 'But remember, success can come in different forms and only you will be the judge of what is success.'

At the time I didn't fully understand what I was scribbling down – I had to concentrate on what he was saying and didn't want to miss anything. But I also wanted to make sure I had something to take away with me to refer back to and reflect on later. With so much going on in my life, there was confusion and I needed focus and clarity from the outside.

My notes were brief.

Blood circulation problem.
Work – overworking. Trying to do too much. Change of career.
Fatigue – need for rest, recovery before moving on.
Relationships – new love but careful, eyes open, not all it seems.
Family bonds strong.

Friends love you and want to help.
Doubtful, fearful – but need to trust and ask for help.
A few years before settled. Complications many.

His predictions about my physical health issues would prove to be spot on – I already had problems with circulation, as did my own mother. I was encouraged about his other messages – especially when he said there would be a positive outlook after the period of turbulence.

'It will never be plain sailing for you,' he said through a smile, 'but you will weather the storms and ultimately find peace.'

'Namaste,' I replied, bowing my head.

25

'Perhaps you need to be a little less worried and defensive, and instead be a little more cunning?'

I arrived back at the office on Monday, healthy and relaxed, alert to a new strain of tension in the air. A senior colleague pulled me into a meeting room to tell me that one of my team had used my absence to cosy up to a consultant working with the other directors, saying she could run things without me.

I was distraught.

I contacted Vanessa, the psychotherapist by the Thames who'd been so helpful before, and went to see her as soon as I could.

'It felt as if I was back at school,' I said. 'One minute I was the happy, confident girl full of fun, the next put back in my place, dejected, unwanted and feeling at the bottom of the class.'

Vanessa asked me to tell her more about those feelings when I was a child. Was there a specific event when I had felt this way?

I told her the story of the Brownies and the Parma Violets.

When I was eight years old, going to 'the Brownies' involved a journey into town on a Tuesday night and the bus back home again. On this particular night we'd played lots of games, new Brownie badges had been awarded and it was still sunny when I emerged from the hall with my chums. Most of them lived locally so walked home. In my Brownie uniform and matching beret with long pigtails hanging down, big bows at the end and wee ears sticking out on each side, I crossed the road to the bus stop. I was a little early and so just had time to take a peek around the corner to see if the Tuck Shop was still open.

It was.

Now the Tuck Shop had all manner of enticing things to buy, such as comics, liquorice, pink shells, squiggly coloured jelly worms, Tutti Fruttis and my most favourite sweeties, Parma Violets. Just right for the ride home. And, like all Scottish children, I had a very sweet tooth. Did you know that the big confectioners often test new chocolate bars, new ice creams, fatty crisps and very sweet sweeties in Scotland because they can get quick, accurate results – because there are so many sweet-eaters and so many other unhealthy things consumed in Scotland?

It's not that you can't get healthy food, it's that we love sweet and fatty foods, having been brought up on them to make up for the bad weather.

I was after a packet of Parma Violets – what an exotic name for those little purple sweets with the most flowery perfumed taste, wrapped in a clear, crunchy-sounding wrapping, twisted at both ends with little dark purple rings. You could pop them in your mouth one at a time (or even two!) and bite, lick or swirl them around your tongue until they melted and your mouth was all violet-coloured, sugary and perfumed. What a special treat for a tired Brownie waiting in the sun for her bus home! And just after that, the bus arrived – right on time.

Perfect.

As I boarded, I pushed my hand into my pocket to get out my bus money. I anxiously felt around for the thruppenny bit that seemed to be missing.

I jumped back off the bus, red-faced, with a slight feeling of panic.

Oh no.

I had spent my bus money on the Parma Violets.

Brownie panic stations.

What to do?

In those days we did not have mobile phones. There was no one I knew nearby (well, I did have one or two chums in the West End but they would be already safely at home). I would have to – yes – walk home on my own, five miles, something I had never done before.

By now the sun was fading.

I began the journey, dragging my feet. I tried to skip. I trudged, looked warily around and behind me as I passed the high-walled Greenock prison with its twisted barbed wire in giant spirals all around the top, and then past the home of the Gibby Gang. I walked along the main road – a lonely Brownie, munching nervously on Parma Violets as she shot looks in all directions, just in case.

'Look, a worried little brown sitting duck, boys!' (I imagined the biggest, scariest members of the Gibby Gang shouting out, as they spied the slow-moving target on Auchmead Road.)

I shivered.

'The wee fair-haired Brownie's petrified – let's go get 'er!' I heard them shout, running towards me (in my head).

I sped up, following the great sweep of the road leading to Burns Cottage, past the high-rise flats and the fish and chip shop, where there were men outside drinking beer and probably worse (oohhhhhh!).

I rushed on, trying not to look over my shoulder as I passed the bungalows and the petrol station – all closed up now, nobody in sight to give me comfort. And now it was dark. There was scant street lighting as we (me and the Parma Violets) began to reach the outskirts of town. Then I came upon the Ravenscraig Hospital – where my grandma had been 'put' years before – 'the loony bin'. Ravenscraig was synonymous with white coats and fearsome screaming.

(Poor Grandma, she gradually went downhill in there, progressively losing her marbles. My lovely dear grandma – the one that had given me Camp coffee in her room and fed me stories of her treasured antiques – was taken away one day.)

'They're coming to take you away, ha ha!' I heard my brother and his school chums chant as I stumbled past.

It was after 9.30 p.m. when I reached the Branchton train station, quite near to home, and I could see right across the big playing fields on the final stretch. The playing field was covered with blaize, a volcanic ashen surface with great big black lumps. It would rip your skin apart if you fell down there. By now I was in tears.

Surely my mum and dad had the police out looking for me by now? Cars and sniffer dogs spread out on patrol to find me holed up somewhere in this most dangerous of towns – at least for lost Brownies.

Tears streamed down my cheeks as I ran towards the house, arms flailing.

A bug hit me and I screamed.

I couldn't see a thing as I scrambled across an ocean of black, scared I would stumble and fall, tripping up on the volcanic ashen surface with big meteoric lumps. If I wasn't careful I might even lose my Brownie beret!

Five minutes later I was at the back door.

I was home.

I tore in to find the whole family, my grandpa, grandma, Glenn, mum and dad gathered together around the fire, engrossed in watching TV. When they saw me they burst out laughing. Even the dog Lassie, jumping up and down, was laughing at me.

I was distraught.

No one had missed me. Absolutely no one.

And when I told them my story, breathless, tearful, my spent bus fare and the Parma Violets, instead of comforting me, they laughed even harder. Only Lassie came over to comfort me. She licked my hands and we cuddled up together by the fire.

卌 卌

Vanessa smiled, and began to laugh.

'The dog again!' she said. 'That must have been terrible for you, Kay, and nobody seemed to care that you were battling the world, all alone.'

And now here I was back again, in that same place all these years later. One minute I was on top, the next cast down, unwanted. It seemed no matter how hard I worked, whenever I was challenged, I couldn't cope. I didn't know how to deal with betrayal.

We were in the middle of the session, discussing possible options, when we were distracted by something outside the window. It was a fox running across the garden. After a few seconds, the fox stopped, turned his head and looked directly at us before jumping over the fence as he fled.

Vanessa smiled. 'There you go, Kay, there's your answer to the conundrum. Perhaps you need to be a little less worried and defensive, and instead be a little more cunning? Perhaps you need to be like the fox there, checking everything out, but keeping his eye on what he's doing, rather than what others are busy with?'

Vanessa was wise.

It certainly made me think about my approach – always jumping to conclusions and blaming myself, being the victim. And so, back at work, instead of launching into an attack, I held back. In only a matter of weeks the problem at work was miraculously gone. I'd said nothing and got on with my work. Then a colleague came up with a clever solution, a win-win to resolve the awkward situation. He proposed a new structure, one that not only recognised essential change to the company, but also recognised my own work and achievements. I was given a new role, a promotion. And the challenger who'd planned the coup?

They left the company within a few months. Phew!

26

'it helped me connect with my inner self more deeply, something most of us never have the chance to do'

I spotted the ad in a magazine and called to make an appointment. I didn't really believe in reincarnation but off I went to my first session of past life regression to see what my past lives might reveal to me. I now had a number of different therapies on the go. As I started one therapy it would quickly lead to another, or a friend would recommend something new, or someone new, knowing I was on a roll, inquisitive, eager and driven. Sometimes it was fun, I was hopeful. Other times I was nervous and afraid – what was I getting into? But I kept going. I wanted to reach my 'new normal' as soon as possible. With all the therapies, each suggesting different solutions, life was a little chaotic at that point. I didn't know this phase would end. I was to lose my job, money would be tight and I'd be forced to slow down. For the moment, however, I was happily juggling.

So here I was in an office near Lancaster Gate, just off Hyde Park, where Lori practised, hidden away from the noise and bustling traffic. The rest of the office was closed for the weekend, so we had the place all to ourselves.

The session began like a meditation, creating a safe 'space' to relax. I lay down on the sofa and shut my eyes, and tried not to think of the tea and cakes to come at Cocomaya just along the road behind Tony Blair's London townhouse.

Lori began to talk to me quietly, 'Now breathe deeply, let everything go heavy in your body, allow yourself to float. You are feeling v-e-r-y relaxed...'

Finally I drifted off. I was half-conscious, but aware of Lori's voice.

Lori asked me to go back to my earliest memory.

Where do you think it is? Who is there? Describe the scene, the weather, what's around you and what are you doing, what do you feel?

Strangely, I seemed to know what to say.

It was like watching a film; the opening scene in *Gladiator* in the wheat fields with tall cypress trees and a farm in the distance. I saw images of biblical times, exotic places and people from Egypt, Mesopotamia or Persia.

I went into a dusty town and watched people in sandals and simple cotton tunics trading goods around a well.

I described what I saw.

I must have been 'under' for twenty minutes, maybe longer, when I heard Lori's soft voice, 'I'm going to count down from five to zero. You'll become aware of your surroundings again, the sights and sounds of your present life, and finally, on the count of zero, you will be fully aware and awake and I want you to open your eyes.'

When I came to, I realised Lori had been taking copious notes, writing everything down.

Lori told me I had been in tears at one point, and it seemed to be a release.

'Do you feel any different?' she asked.

'I feel calm, and it's exciting to think that I had a life back in ancient, biblical times.'

'Yes, Persia,' she purred, 'and Mesopotamia and Egypt.'

Lori told me about her experience of Egypt the previous year – I was so interested (given my other connection with Egypt) that she offered to connect me with the leader, Chris, to see if he might have space on his shamanic trip to the Sahara Desert and the Pyramids.

I didn't feel any immediate difference as I wrote her a cheque but I was assured that the session would have an influence at some point in the coming months. Lori promised to finish off my 'regression notes' and send them on. She wouldn't keep a copy.

When the notes finally arrived I couldn't make much sense of them. It all seemed a bit of a jumble, just like my life, and in the cold light of day, a little far-fetched and 'out there'. But, I loved the guided meditation, it helped me connect with my inner self more deeply, something most of us never have the chance to do – and some of us will never do. It isn't the end of the story either. Past life can delve into many more areas that you can visit like a time traveller; just ask and it can be done.

Most important of all, it was to lead to my shamanic trip to Egypt – a unique experience, as it would turn out.

27

'It was intense. It had a profound effect on me as it clearly did for the others. We felt very closely bonded after sharing that experience'

Lots of therapies tell you that acceptance is part of your 'road to personal enlightenment' and that it's up to you to change the way you think. Van Morrison even wrote a song about the spiritual quest; singing about 'non-attachment', and being 'in the here and now', of 'one hand clapping'.

I have to admit it can all become quite confusing – reality being an illusion and transcendental mind consciousness being the thing that's important.

But I was gradually learning to go with the flow.

And I still wasn't done.

So the offer of a deeper journey into the subconscious – a shamanic retreat in Egypt, seventeen days, much of it out in the desert with a small group, an experienced practitioner and a spiritual quest – was irresistible.

I rang and spoke to the leader, Chris, who seemed enthusiastic, and surprised by the novelty of my unexpected call and my Scottish accent.

I signed up on the spot.

̶H̶H̶ ̶H̶H̶

The cloudless sky, an impenetrable blue, stretched across the horizon and high up, where I was headed, sat the sun, a great dazzling cross of white light.

After a long day of driving, the five jeeps had come to a stop in a small semicircle in the sands.

I grabbed my iPod and ran barefoot away from the sound of German voices and unpacking. I ran as fast as I could, up and down across the dunes, sometimes sprinting, sometimes skipping and sometimes spinning around. Occasionally I'd stop to look back at my footprints in the sand, already filling in around the edges so that there was nothing but a line of dimples outlining my path back towards camp.

Finally, I stopped and dropped to the ground, lying on my back, arms and legs outstretched, breathless, heart pumping, looking up at the empty sky.

Peace at last.

Alone in the desert.

I lay there, listening to today's track: 'Dunia', repeated over and over until I had my fill – it made a change from the Native American flutes, Tibetan chants, whale song, Pat Metheny, my favourite gayatri mantra from Lex van Someren or the guitar soundscapes of 'Aerial Boundaries'. The tracks all made me feel good and less anxious, as if I was headed somewhere, with purpose.

London and my job were far away. I was missing some important work meetings and a special event too: I had received a call to say I was 'Legacy Champion of the Year' and could I come to the ceremony in November to receive the award from Olympic legend, Dame Kelly Holmes?

Oh no!

I would be far away running up and down sand dunes in my bare feet.

I was pushing myself, forcing myself to leave my comfort zone.

I was sorry to miss the event but it couldn't be helped.

Instead, here I was in the Sahara with a group of strangers, travelling cross-country in rickety buses, and jeeps, taking it all in; the Pyramids, caves, bleak lunar landscapes, rocks, fossils and, somewhat bewilderingly, seashells – millions of seashells scattered about the desert where once there were oceans. Sleeping under the stars, all wrapped up in a spiritual blanket of shamanism, I'd close my eyes feeling utterly content and at one with the world – what more could you want?

Back home, I had certainly become more chilled. One morning I'd rushed in to join the weekly business development meeting, upbeat, well prepared but uncharacteristically late, carrying bags and coffee with sunglasses still on. In the gloom of the meeting room, I clumsily dropped my things onto the table and took my place, apologising. One of the new bosses who didn't know me stopped talking, midstream, unsmiling, then continued. A couple of people in the team glanced at me and chuckled as they looked up from the long, detailed spreadsheet of financials.

Yes, I was exploring new avenues, including my discovery of the myriad therapies that occupied much of my free time, and spoke about these openly to close colleagues (possibly a mistake).

Perhaps word had got round that I was off on a 'Shamanic trip to Egypt'.

Geez, she's finally lost it.

Who knew?

Maybe I had.

But it didn't mean I couldn't do a good job.

Yet I was changing. I was less serious, more vulnerable, perhaps more easy to criticise or worse, a perfect sitting duck. Had I changed so much that they could simply point the finger and say, '*It's time for her to go*'?

༒ ༒

Lying in the sand, I slowly opened my eyes and removed the earpieces. Across the dunes, faintly at first, came the sound of a distant horn. It was Chris, the group leader, blowing on his ancient ram's horn to call us back to the campfire. Some of the group had taken a short stroll together, or gone off to choose their spot for the night, dropping their sleeping bags in the dunes.

Darkness falls quickly in the desert and, as I stood up, I realised that if it weren't for the faint flickering fire in the distance, I'd have been stranded. I began to run back, up and down the dunes towards the campfire – it had taken me a long time to get this far and now I felt scared, unable to see the fire until I reached the top of the next dune. My legs were pounding and I stumbled occasionally, guided only by the stars.

When I eventually arrived, the group was halfway through the meal. The Egyptian driver, Ammon, looked a little concerned, but the rest laughed and welcomed me back.

My fellow travellers included a group of trainee NLP master practitioners – Chris led these groups every year for people wanting to be like him, professional rather than hobbyists like me. I was about to be steeped in ancient shamanic techniques and surrounded by some very serious students, adventurous 'self-explorers'. No stone would be left unturned. I was in good hands, it seemed.

Back in Berlin, the group had been attending a series of workshops with the leader, Chris, who was an accomplished self-development guru. He was well-travelled, interesting and good fun and we were enthralled by his observations about life and the world. When he wasn't giving a 'talk' or lecture in German to his followers, he spoke in English, which everyone understood.

He'd find time to come to talk to me, sitting down next to me on the bus as we travelled to our next destination.

I was fascinated – he said shamanism had been an integral part of the self-understanding of people since the beginning of mankind. But his brand of shamanism wasn't associated with any particular belief system – he told us it's possible for anyone to use the essence of shamanic knowledge. The trip was intended to stimulate our 'neglected' side and to explore different techniques to reach altered states of consciousness. It was to be a journey through Egypt as much as a journey into our inner selves.

There were visits to mosques, spice traders and fabric sellers in the fabulous bazaars. There were group meditations; once on a high rocky plateau deep in the mountains, all of us spaced out in a wide circle, feeling the special energy of the place, taking in the sun, a light breeze and a few sounds. There was chanting, there was traditional music – ancient dance rituals and Bedouin folksong – and then music of a different kind, inside one of Egypt's best-known pyramids. Chris had arranged a special visit to Giza, the oldest and largest of the pyramids. We were excited to learn that, at a pre-arranged time, our Egyptian hosts were to throw out all the brief-stay tourists and pack them off with their cameras back to their air-conditioned coaches, leaving the entire Great Pyramid to ourselves. And we'd go all the way to the centre.

The descent was very steep. Deep inside the labyrinth of tunnels, we had hundreds of steps to negotiate, everyone bent double in the tiny space. It was narrow too – just a four-foot square tunnel with only occasional rest spots where you could stand up and stretch. We stuck together all the way up and down through the many passageways, through the Grand Gallery, to the Queen's Chamber, then further still, now ascending the steps until finally all of us, one by one, squeezed through a small opening in the rock leading into the pyramid's central space to see the King's Chamber and granite sarcophagus.

It was claustrophobic, dusty, airless and made worse when we heard the lights were to be switched off and the noisy mechanical ventilation shut down so that we could experience this unique place in all its glory.

We lay down with the top of our heads touching the outer wall of the great room, feet towards the centre.

There was complete silence, complete darkness.

After we'd settled, Chris took us on a journey – a shamanic meditation. He took a few minutes to help us relax and breathe more slowly, his voice echoing gently around the chamber. Our eyes were open, straining into the darkness as he spoke, his voice bounced off the granite walls.

'Stay with me, listening to my voice, as you drift and float, further and further away. You should begin to be comfortable with the idea of leaving your body, drifting up and coming back like waves. Use the energy of this "resonator room" and go to the far reaches of our universe if you wish. You can easily go to the furthest limits of our energetic universe. Explore, download, whatever amount of energy or whatever information or whatever amount of development you need.

'After this experience no matter how faint it might seem for you now, life is never going to be the same again. Later, you might wonder how things are suddenly aligning in your life, why random events or coincidences are happening to you. This is not hypnosis, this is not a hypnotic command – no – I know from the deepest point of my heart that they will be happening to you. As you start enjoying this everlasting moment of tranquility and silence in here – and maybe for the first time in your life – you can experience total silence.'

We listened. Nothing. Total silence.

Then, after some time lying there together in that sound-less space, an eerie and ethereal music started up from the darkness – a weird and wonderful melody, it was a single voice that sounded like a choir. Throat singing, vocal chords producing multiple harmonics, evocative and strange. It was supernatural and thrilling. Many minutes passed. It could have been hours. I felt far away. When the heavenly music eventually stopped, the final sound echoing around the chamber for some time, there was a long pause before Chris continued.

'Just listen to the faint regular breathing, listen to your own heartbeat and you might become aware that your eyelids are slowly, slowly, becoming even heavier. Let go and yeeeeeesssss, take that deep, deep breath in' (sound of Chris whooshing in breath), 'then "ooooo" and out.' Another long pause ...

'And now I want everybody to join in a very quiet OM – at a certain point you will hear my voice again, calling for silence once more. Find with your OM the resonance frequency of this room – because the resonance frequency of this room has certain qualities, acoustically and energetically, that are unique.

'So let's start OMMMMMM [singing] – all joining in [sound echoing around].'

It was intense. It had a profound effect on me as it clearly did for the others. We felt very closely bonded after sharing that experience.

As we started the long walk back, out through the tunnels and passageways, we felt our energies renewed, and although it was a tiring climb back, when we finally emerged into the bright sunlight, in some way we knew we'd experienced ourselves and life for the first time.

On the drive back to Cairo I felt a true sense of peace, but there was still one last stop – a sweeping landscape of rocks and cliffs with black and white sands stretching down towards the valley, winding together like two rivers, then disappearing into the horizon. It felt like a sacred place with extraordinary sculpted rock formations. Chris led the group off towards a white chalk and clay escarpment. We saw that the white carpet was made up of thousands of tiny disc-shaped shells several layers deep and stretching for hundreds of yards. We picked them up to examine them more closely. Chris encouraged everyone to take some. He was going to take them home to make buttons for his jackets and encouraged us to fill our pockets.

I thought I had better not.

I loved looking at them, marvelling at their beauty, as they glinted in the sunshine, but I would not take any. Best to see them where they belonged. I had seen beautiful things like this before on my travels and learnt through bitter personal experience that it was a pointless exercise for me to remove these precious things.

If this continued, it would only be a matter of years, and just a few more groups like this one, each taking a tiny number of these pretty trinkets lying on the ground, before very soon, nothing would remain – the place would be denuded of fossils and there would be nothing left for anyone to enjoy or contemplate. Worse still, when they found their way back home (if they did indeed survive the journey intact), they no longer had the same value in their new setting. At best, they would be put on display or kept in a drawer, but at some point, they would be thrown away. Lost forever and lost to the world.

I still wonder if Chris made his buttons.

28

'one day I'd skipped right across the black hole without a moment's thought. It no longer troubled me'

My therapist Vanessa had always encouraged me to keep going even when I felt stuck and unable to avoid repeating 'negative cycles of behaviour'. She said the journey towards healing was a gradual one.

'It can't be rushed.'

Yet I was becoming impatient.

I wanted to find a new level of stability in my personal life.

I'd been made redundant and had decided to take the plunge and set up a new company, but despite securing a few good pieces of consultancy, the work wasn't regular. I didn't have a steady income. Things were painfully slow.

Vanessa described the process.

'Imagine you need to move forward. In front of you is a great black hole. At first you walk straight towards it, into it, almost compelled. Over time, you learn to recognise the hazard for what it is – remember, you went back to that man many times, then one day you didn't. You just have to begin to find ways to avoid walking into the black hole. The more you acknowledge your repeating behaviours, the inevitable consequences and negative outcomes, the more you will begin to move away from what was once unavoidable. And one day, almost without thinking, you will suddenly discover that you have managed to walk around the problem. You will have no regrets and no more need to fall into that bleak and lonely place. You will do it, but it will take time.'

So I kept going.

It made sense.

I remembered the day when, for the third time, the psychic gave me the same message about the 'man of your destiny'. It was an important chance to step around that particular obstacle.

And one day I'd skipped right across the black hole without a moment's thought. It no longer troubled me. And then eventually the black hole disappeared altogether.

29

'In that moment, after listening to all the other sad stories, I suddenly realised for the first time how much I had been loved'

I walked up to the microphone and began to talk. The story was simple: how my mother always brought me a scarf when she came to collect me from Glasgow Airport. While it didn't sound like much, it had suddenly struck me how much she'd cared.

But it was too late to tell her, to acknowledge her love.

She was gone.

There she would be with my father, waiting opposite arrivals so that the moment the automatic doors opened we could see each other. She'd be wearing a big radiant pink lipstick grin and ready with that scarf.

My husband and I always looked pale when we emerged, she said. As usual, down in London we had been tearing around, working too hard, flying up and down to Scotland each week.

At first we had been looking for a house, then we were buying a house, a detached villa on the Clyde, then we were doing it up, then we were trying to live in it as much as possible, when not away on business or on holidays to far-flung places, while also holding down careers in London. Now we were finally in a regular routine – sorting out the gardening, the new furniture, the building works (an indoor pool), the leaks in the roof, the new hand-crafted wooden gates, building a garage and then rushing back down to London for the working week.

We never took a break.

Apart from our special holidays, ever since our honeymoon, a cheetah safari in Africa, we had become interested in wildlife, different cultures, conservation – and it started us on quite an adventure. We did everything from whale watching in Alaska and the far east of Russia to coastal trips looking for penguins in Patagonia, polar bears in the Arctic tundra, gorillas in Rwanda, pandas in China, the list went on. But even those holidays were a race, a marathon, and while exhilarating, also tiring.

My parents worried. Yes, it was lovely that we were doing all those things, and juggling lucrative work in London with a new home in Scotland where we planned to retire early, but we always looked tired. And we always seemed to forget simple things, such as how much colder it was in Scotland. But Mum always remembered and brought me a scarf, which she'd wrap around my neck the minute we said hello.

卌 卌

In that moment, after listening to all the other sad stories, I suddenly realised for the first time how much I had been loved. I had been cared for all along, and this simple, small gesture of my mother's, who I knew found it difficult to be openly warm and loving towards me (she wasn't of the generation to be tactile or demonstrative), revealed her true feelings. I don't know why it was important to tell this to a room full of strangers, but it was what came out. The tears came next. My voice was unsteady, trembling; it was emotional, this sudden, public recognition of something that had never occurred to me when my mother was alive.

During her fight with cancer, no one really thought about feelings. Not until it was over.

All our efforts were focused on protecting her, helping Dad deal with this terrible relentless battle, which he was struggling to cope with, taking Mum to hospital and waiting for the results. Chemotherapy, radiotherapy, operations, reversal operations, unpleasant paraphernalia to deal with at home, blood tests, endless medication, nurses visits, hospital stays – different hospitals, ambulances at the door, nee naw, nee naw... She needed a carrier bag to transport her records and GP notes around. And then, after four long years, the cancer suddenly spread. It appeared in new places. She was in the specialist radiotherapy hospital in Glasgow when the doctors suddenly announced they could no longer justify subjecting her to more treatment. She was brought back home to Greenock.

The nurses told her to lie flat – they told her off for trying to sit up, even when she was uncomfortable lying down. One disgruntled nurse threw her painkillers on her bed after I made a fuss – Mum had been waiting patiently in agonising pain while they had a meeting. She was distraught, and helpless. They didn't seem to understand her constant need for pain relief. She looked at us, trying to look fine, knowing she would prefer us not to look at her with that terrified expression, but how can you act and look fine with all that going on, letting her down, unable to help? She had to be strong, despite what was happening inside. The cancer was unstoppable. She was moved to a hospice. At least they understood pain relief. They made her as comfortable as they could. The atmosphere was peaceful, but by that time we only had weeks, and then days – that last week I lay my head next to hers on the pillow and sang 'The Dicky Bird Hop' and then 'Step We Gaily', the chorus to one of her favourite Scottish folk tunes – she tried to join in but with the morphine, it was difficult.

And then, that last day, while my brother had stepped out for a few minutes, and I was sitting by her bed with Dad and my husband, she suddenly breathed a last, long, deep sigh and was gone. At first we just looked at each other blankly.

'She's gone, Kay,' Dad said, looking at me, his voice thick with disbelief.

It was shocking how quickly it was all over.

A horrible chasm opened up, a great empty hole that could never be filled.

卌 卌

People in the group were looking at me with red eyes, dabbing their faces with paper hankies. I kept talking through the tears, crying in front of everyone. I tailed off. It was time to get off the stage and let the next person 'share'.

Everyone was there for different reasons but all of them searching for answers.

Different cultures, backgrounds, motivations, stories, but the same desire to share. There was a real feeling of togetherness, we were united by our collective pain. It was cathartic for everyone to get it out, to feel the sympathy of others and realise that you weren't alone, that others were suffering too.

This so-called 're-education' was a new experience. Laura had recommended it after a homeopathy session and gave me the newspaper article to keep until I was ready. I felt strong enough, motivated enough to go, finally. This was the introductory session of the 'course'.

We were told, tantalisingly, that some people on the course have 'enormous breakthroughs', their lives had been transformed and some had achieved incredible success. Only later was I to find out that this introductory session – a non-stop stint of several hours – was only the start, the tip of the iceberg, the baring-of-the-soul part. As the stories continued, there was some laughter, but more often we heard gasps. There was sympathy but also shock at the honesty and drama relayed in these personal experiences. People who had never spoken in public before, perhaps encouraged by the honesty of others, left their seats and joined the queue of individuals ready to speak.

Compared with psychotherapy or healing, this was very public.

Some people never came back. Others, like me, couldn't wait for the next session – a full weekend, three long days, morning till night with just a few breaks for food or homework, not a moment to spare, completely stuffed with things to do, and reflect on.

I would be back home late, then up early the next morning (we also had homework in those few short hours away from the conference centre). It was gruelling work. At the end of the course we were given a 'qualification' which allowed us to move on to the next, higher level courses – the promise of more – not just a new you, but a better you, a more success-ful you. Finally, here, your true leadership qualities would be revealed.

I eventually did four full weekend sessions.

I was surprised, then, to be asked to leave early, just a matter of hours before the end of the third and final day on one of those weekends. According to one of the 'leaders', I wasn't complying. I wasn't on message, I was resisting (how anyone can see you as resistant after putting up with all those hours of purgatory is extraordinary).

Although it was obviously a terrible sin and I felt like one of the untouchables as I picked up my coat to leave (watched by all the believers), I was allowed to do a re-sit (without paying).

I felt bad. Perhaps I was just sick of all the self-criticism, which frankly felt like torture.

But I still wanted to succeed so I told myself: 'it's just a another thirty-five hour weekend to get through. I can do it and, this time, with the benefit of repeating the experience, I know not to try and resist, just go with the flow.'

On the first proper weekend course we all expected more of the same – more revelations as on the introductory session. But, in fact, after that first night things would change. Those of us who signed up for the full weekend were in for a surprise. Rather than validating our stories, in the follow-up we were told it was precisely those stories that were holding us back in life – our stories had become self-fulfilling prophesies. It might have been a couple of minor incidents in our early childhood, but these incidents or 'life stories' had stayed with us for years and had ended up defining our lives.

How ridiculous.

We all agreed.

So what was my story?

I thought about it – ah yes, I wasn't loved, and then there were the shaming Sunday morning quiz sessions (I'll show them!), the constant put-downs (never again!), my father's comments (no man will treat me like that!), the fact that I wasn't really wanted (boo hoo): Mum didn't even want children and she'd sacrificed an exciting career for us and never fulfilled her true potential (and so I had never had children but just focused on my job) – and it was all our fault (sob, sob, life was really terrible, wasn't it? I didn't ask to be born!) – oh yes, it all came out.

But now with the help of the re-education I was happy to see if I could wipe the slate clean, to free myself from old thinking and move on. A rebirth. We were all up for that, of course.

The days were long.

I was so tired when I got home that I fell straight into bed and slept like a log. I dragged myself up the next day for more of the same. During the day we had lectures on how resistant we were, how we had to show commitment and integrity by making the calls to people we'd 'wronged' in the past. We were given exercises to work on in groups about being authentic and not shirking our duties, then in the evening, we were let out for an hour and a half – for a change of scenery (we were still working) as we ate together in local fry-up cafes or cheap Chinese restaurants, discussing, planning and preparing presentations on goodness knows what.

It was confrontational stuff. Harsh. Once we'd acknowledged that we were flawed and living our lives through these 'stories', we had to talk to friends, colleagues and family about what we were doing. Imagine having to call people and apologise for something you had done years ago, perhaps things that had harmed them or things we had promised to do, but not delivered upon.

I had to call up my much-loved babysitter Margaret, using the slightly stilted language that we had been 'taught', apologising for being a difficult and troubled child: 'It was just that I felt isolated, lesser, somehow, unloved,' I explained.

In fact, she was so happy to hear from me, she said, 'That's not true, Kay. You were the most lovely, sweet little girl, always smiling, fun, a lovely wee thing!'

Other calls didn't go so well. Some people I tried to 'enlist', friends, began to worry about me.

'Great, Kay, glad you're doing this, but it's not for me – and are you sure it's good for you? What does it all mean?'

'What's it called?'

'A re-education? I'm forty-five! I don't want to start to re-educate myself at my age.'

If we made the calls *correctly*, it would have the added benefit of demonstrating the positive power of the re-education programme – selling to potential new joiners. We became fully paid-up evangelists for the 'movement'. I wasn't very good at that part. Besides, what did signing people up have to do with me?

Thumbing through my list of contacts, I realised that I'd lost touch with a whole swathe of friends following my divorce.

I didn't want to contact them.

I had lots of acquaintances but it was excruciating to call them and involve them in my 're-education'.

And yet we kept hearing about the successes – unnamed people that had sudden dramatic personal discoveries. You could see those in the group that had experienced this – they returned to the session the next day beaming, knowing, satisfied.

Others, like me, found the whole thing profoundly diminishing. But I wasn't a quitter, I had to finish what I'd started. Somehow I forced myself to jump through hoops. Not only that, for one of those four weekend courses I flew to the US. Geez.

When you first signed up for a course, you signed up for the complete set of dates, as advertised.

As you'd expect, occasionally someone couldn't make the date, 'Why can't you come? Can't you juggle commitments to make this happen? You know that in life you can always do whatever you want if you really want to do it. It's only your lack of commitment that's getting in the way, your resistance, you can easily shuffle off this problem if you want. Show us your commitment to your future and your re-education,' they'd say cheerfully.

When it came to my turn to have to miss one of the weekends, it was unavoidable. I had to go and see my father in hospital.

'You'll have to find an alternative session, Kay, or you won't complete the course – somehow you have to make it work. How about going elsewhere if you really can't make it? There are re-education sessions taking place all over the world, all the time. If you can't attend in London, you can attend elsewhere. Here's the list of places and times in all the different countries – that help?' he said, smiling.

I looked at the long list of worldwide re-education centres together with dates they were running my course. Seemed a bit extreme to travel.

'Where are you going that weekend?' he pressed. 'Are you in one of these places? Can you attend a session while you are away there?'

'No, I'm just going up to Scotland.'

But there was no way out either. There was always someone on the team ready to help sort out any problem that you might have.

He watched me as I looked through the schedules again – I had to fit my session into a certain timescale. There was one that I could possibly make in Amsterdam, not too far.

'There's one in Amsterdam, but I don't speak Dutch?'

'No problem, they're all in English,' he said.

Then I saw Philadelphia.

It fitted my schedule. I had never been to Philadelphia. It might be good to see how the sessions were run in a different country. Americans were famously good at communication, sharing – they were so confident – they never had a problem with 'going with the flow'. So it was that I fixed up a trip to Philadelphia and soon I was flying off for a long weekend in Pennsylvania to be with my American re-education chums.

30

'I see you are in pain. Your lover is no longer with you. He is going, retreating, drifting away. You are unhappy, alone.
You want him back. Yes?'

Philadelphia was lovely and as it happened, the Americans were much more relaxed about the re-education. Compared to the angst-ridden Brits who all took it so seriously, this was a doddle. They didn't seem to bother much about the homework – we went for a meal and had a nice chat. They gave me tips on what to see downtown and one of the girls met me for lunch in a farmers' market.

I had a day to myself before flying back and I took a walk in the sun in the pretty part of town with street names such as Church and Parrish, Pine and Larchwood. I did the sights, the symbols of freedom – the giant Liberty Bell, a tour round Independence Hall – and kept on walking until I found myself down near the port with its rows of buildings blackened with industrial grime and broad stone steps leading up to the doorways. I had been listening to my music, eating a giant ice cream when I spotted a house with 'Tarot, Clairvoyant Healer, Love Spells, Black Magic, Voodoo' painted in red on the window.

I couldn't resist.

Inside was a dark room with a curtained-off area in one corner. It was eerie with an oily smell and candles burning, strange objects lying about made of straw and bone, and some worn leather-bound books.

The curtain was suddenly swept aside as an African turban emerged from the darkness, followed by the bosomy figure of a woman stuffed into a yellow and black patterned dress. She was incredibly old with a wizened face and a gold tooth that caught the light. Her jewellery rattled – chains and leather hoops hung around her neck, gold bangles all the way up her forearm and rings on every finger. One was a skull.

'Come and sit,' she said in a wheezy voice, indicating a bench just inside.

She shuffled backwards, falling into an enormous carved wooden chair, with a high back and a stack of puffed-up cushions that deflated slowly as she settled into position.

She immediately began some sort of evocation, 'I call on the spirits...'

I looked at her wrinkled face, eyes shut, in the flickering candlelight and inhaled the heavy smell of wax and rose scented perfume. It was stuffy in the small room.

'I see you are in pain. Your lover is no longer with you. He is going, retreating, drifting away. You are unhappy, alone. You want him back. Yes?'

I was taken by surprise. Was she reading my mind, or did she say this to every stranger coming through her door?

'Well, I haven't met anyone else yet but if it's who I think you're meaning – someone from the past – then I don't think it's possible to bring it back or even if I'd want him now.'

Was he going to come back? Oh no, I couldn't start with all that again.

It was becoming stifling in that hot room.

I couldn't breathe and began to feel uncomfortable.

She kept on, words tumbling from her mouth.

I sighed, loudly.

I think she must have heard. She opened her eyes and looked directly into my face.

'If you *really* want this man, you must do as I say. Go and buy two outfits, a wedding dress for you and a wedding suit for him. You must take these things home and keep them side by side. These are the words you must repeat while burning this red candle that I give you. For twenty days without fail you will continue. If you do this, the man will come back. Out of the blue, he will return and he will stay, the decision will be made and he will be yours forever.'

Ridiculous, who would do that? How could I even respond to that?

She could see my hesitation.

'You aren't serious about this man if you don't do as I say. That would be the proof that you really do want him.'

'Really? No thanks,' I said as I got up and raced out of there as quickly as I could.

꜒꜒꜒ ꜒꜒꜒

Back in London, it was back to the grind.

We were told to pick a project and show our absolute commitment to it in the same way we had done the re-education work. I decided to supercharge my efforts on the Olympic legacy by enrolling as many people as I could to make it happen. It meant working even harder. We were encouraged to be 'unstoppable' (that suited me well, as that's what I'd been doing all my life).

Then after the fourth course, I'd had enough. I'd thrown myself into the programme, experienced the pain and now wanted out. It was hard extricating myself. People still on the course called me up to persuade me to come back. I had to stop answering.

Then they emailed.

Kay, we're worried about you.

I was done. Enough.

Leave me alone.

31

"The more I thought about it, the more I realised that cutting myself off had become a constant theme in my life"

I always enjoyed travelling solo. Even as a student when I'd decide to go on a trip, I used to take off on my own – the more adventurous the trip, the better. One year I travelled through India and Nepal. I was very careful about when I went out, but I was still a petite blonde in male dominated cultures, unmarried and travelling alone.

Later, I went to the US and Canada for eight weeks. I carefully plotted my bicoastal trip across America on Greyhound buses, stopping in Cheyenne, Wichita, Cincinnati, Sioux Falls, Phoenix, Albuquerque, Death Valley, Bryce Canyon and Colorado Springs.

My mother was very keen for me to meet my delightful extended family, descended from Scots who had emigrated to the US and settled there. Visiting adorable Ralph and Larry was very important (my mum's second cousins twice removed). At other times, I'd hang out with people I met on the bus – born-again Christians proffering gifts, an American bagpipe player from St Louis wearing a kilt (!), loud South Africans, a geeky guy from Holland.

But more often than not, I was happy to sit alone, travelling hundreds of miles, watching the incredible landscapes fly by – the endless green plains with bison grazing, wheat fields and blue skies, great cliffs of white stone, towering rocks and boulders, canyons, lakes and dams. We sped through the gold-mining towns, the rust belt industrial and modern high-rise cities with gleaming architecture.

Now, many years later, I'm more cautious. I'd found that yoga retreats suited me, combining travel, spiritual pursuits and a safe environment – usually all women – and you could still find some opportunities to be alone if you wanted to be.

HH HH

I met Dee on an all-girl yoga retreat. Dee was dedicated to a career in yoga while her famous husband ran an astrology shop in Covent Garden. The house and estate chosen for the yoga retreat was a vast Jacobean-style property with carved stonework, grand staircases, dark wood panelling and enormous rooms, set in sprawling grounds with lots of mature trees. Apparently the merchant banker Robert Fleming had once owned the place and his grandson Ian Fleming (of James Bond fame) spent much of his childhood there. It was now a palliative care nursing home and training centre, which explained the tranquility.

In the mornings before breakfast we'd do silent walking meditations, snaking around the grounds in single file behind our leader, and apart from lunch, the rest of the day was spent in almost continuous yoga practice. The evenings were for relaxation and we'd congregate in the lounge, in comfortable old armchairs and flowery-covered sofas. Discussions were about yoga as the others were teaching diploma students and had homework to prepare.

I listened with interest and loved the leader Mena's approach to the ancient practice – she was a former chair of The British Wheel of Yoga and gave us a thorough grounding. But she had many other strings to her bow – hypnotherapy, psychotherapy, reiki and meditation. She was very smart and at somewhere between sixty-five and seventy extremely fit and supple; an example to us all of the effectiveness of yoga and how it can keep you young.

I liked the way she explained everything, keeping it simple, and demonstrated the difficult postures with the greatest of ease. She was elegant and had incredible poise even when balancing the weight of her whole body on one arm.

One night I sat next to Dee and discussed our interest in alternative therapies. On hearing about her deep involvement in astrology, I asked if she would do my chart.

I didn't know anything about astrology but I was curious to have what she called a 'birth chart interpretation'.

Dee had a formal training in astrology and believed in its power and authenticity. She said she would be in touch.

I had no idea how much work goes into a birth chart but was about to find out. Having provided the exact time of day and place of my birth, my own personal chart arrived a few weeks later.

It was two and a half pages long. I read through it carefully. It was fascinating.

At the end, Dee had written, 'Do let me know if you want to meet to discuss – much love, light and blessings to you, dearest Kay. Hari om.'

It was packed full of interesting observations and insights. It also posed some tricky questions about my childhood and family. There was so much that resonated with me. It seemed to get right to the heart of my past family background as well as my present situation.

〰 〰

Once I'd had time to digest it – rereading it many times – we arranged to meet for a coffee.

'Hello, Kay, how's the yoga doing?' Dee greeted me warmly.

We talked together as she led me through to her kitchen, where the documents were already spread out across the table.

She had gone to the trouble of printing out a laminated copy of my astrology 'wheel' so that I could keep it safe. It looked beautiful with all the Egyptian symbols, zodiac signs and planets and it had a set of criss-cross lines in the lower left-hand side of the central circle – this was the 'shape' of my chart captured at the exact time of my birth.

'It certainly seems like an important time for you right now, Kay,' Dee began. 'Lots of change and, as you said when we met at the yoga retreat, not necessarily the happiest of times for you and it looks set to be a long haul for the next six years or so until everything gets sorted out.'

That was a blow.

'Something might happen in relation to the Olympic Games, I suppose,' I suggested.

'Possibly,' she nodded. 'On the positive side, it looks like new beginnings are on their way, and a chance for renewal.'

It was time to interpret those thin ruled lines.

'Something quite traumatic happened around the time of your birth – do you have any idea what that was?' 'No, I don't remember anyone ever mentioning anything.'

'You might want to try to find out from someone in the family – your father, perhaps – see if they can remember? It was quite catastrophic but it has meant that when you're faced with setbacks – and you have many – you in fact handle them rather well. It's not the end of the world, it's simply something you deal with and then start again, but this time moving forward with greater strength and wisdom, allowing you to rise from the ashes like a phoenix.'

I smiled.

I liked the idea of rebirth despite it originating in a disaster.

Dee wanted to know more about my parents.

'Was your mother happy, Kay? Did she bear the brunt of bringing up the family? I see exhaustion and frustration as if she sacrificed some of her own desires to keep things going. Perhaps she was unfulfilled in some way?'

I nodded, picturing her rushing around, cigarette in hand, organising everyone. She once talked of a job she might have had in Germany (she was all ready to go) but then Dad came along, quickly followed by children, which put a stop to all that.

'And what of your father, Kay – it isn't an entirely clear picture, he doesn't figure much – was he absent most of the time? I nodded again. 'More importantly, has this had a bearing on your own relationships with men – distant, fleeting – you said this was a problem when we met.'

I thought about it – yes, my husband was often away on business – Hong Kong for two years, then commuting up and down to Scotland and only back at weekends, not helped by my own unsociable shift work, and, of course there was Mr Egypt – so yes, distant, fleeting.

The week my mother died, I was told by a friend of hers that she'd once tried to end it all.

Really?

I was shocked.

My mother held everything together. Alone. For several years my father tried to find a job closer to home, giving up his beloved deep sea career in order to support Mum with the family. But in the meantime, she had more than just my brother and me to look after – my dad's frail and ageing mother as well as a patient from the nearby nursing home when it closed down. Sounds quite overwhelming for a mum on her own.

For a while after Dad returned from sea, he worked as a salesman but he was still away, travelling around Scotland as he waited patiently for a commission on the Clyde.

And later Mum was often frustrated, anxious and battling with male authority figures at work. She was a natural feminist although I don't think she would ever have wanted that label. Through her love of sports (golf, tennis, badminton, sailing, curling, the list goes on) she became involved in ladies committees and did lots of charity work. In this, she often came up against male chauvinism and hated the men's club mentality – the segregation of ladies' and men's areas in the golf clubs was a particular bugbear, the women's areas being smaller and confined to the edges of the clubhouse, the men maintaining their power and control from their mini fiefdoms in the main club rooms and bars.

As a result of her antagonism (she wasn't quiet) and proactive (and successful) efforts to change the status quo (women now had free-run of all the clubhouse areas), she often found herself unpopular with the men. They didn't like her interference, it was unwelcome and they resisted strongly at first. Sound familiar? Eventually my mother would win and the other women would congratulate her, but it was heavy going and took its toll.

Even at work, where she was PA to the MD, it was only when she left suddenly (after having had enough, feeling isolated and unappreciated) that her work and contribution was recognised. The boss called and called to ask her to help him sort out the growing mess. Some of the other male bosses – they were all male – said she wasn't important but as soon as she left they realised she was responsible for so many crucial arrangements for the company – including securing Canadian wheat (at the best price) and cherries (only the best) for the baker's famous Black Forest gateaux (really sophisticated in the mid 1970s).

She was an inspiration, although I didn't know it at the time. But I took on board the lesson that you had to fight to get what you wanted, that there were many enemies (especially men) and that you had to keep going, no matter how painful it might be. I also learned that a career could get you places, not children (she'd had to give up on her own dreams to look after the family), and that flightiness and overt femininity were not your friends. Hard work was what mattered.

I told Dee that I was like Mum and that her astrology reading had made me reflect on just how much she had done, and that I had inherited her aversion to male authority and superiority (whether earned or otherwise).

It reminded me of the story about Nelson Mandela, an interesting example.

\#\#\# \#\#\#

Jonathan and I had been waiting in the airport lounge at Glasgow. It was our weekly trip back to London after another happy weekend in the big house. The sun had sparkled on the estuary waves, lapping towards the shore, rocking the black and white ducks at the start of yet another perfect day. We had left the drive to the airport until the very last minute.

At the airport, we were expecting the usual routine, the rush to check in and secure a seat in the front rows (hopefully right behind business class so that we could dash off to the Tube at the other end rather than waiting for the tedious row-by-row exit process of glum-faced travellers at Heathrow).

Sitting in the lounge, I was busy people watching, sipping my tea, while Jonathan was buried in his newspaper, his fingers crawling up the edges – crab-like, turning the next page slowly, absorbing every detail, not missing a thing.

Something caught my eye on the other side of the lounge, a faint flurry of activity, a change from the general rumble of low-level whispered conversation and flight announcements. Suddenly the huddle opened up and a man came striding towards us with great purpose followed by his entourage. He stopped to acknowledge a comment from one of the waiting passengers and gave a brief wave, then to my surprise, started walking straight towards me. As he approached, I gently nudged Jonathan's arm.

'Jonathan. It's Nelson Mandela.'

'What?' he retorted, without looking up.

I jabbed him again, this time more sharply, slightly crushing one side of his newspaper.

'Jonathan, it's bloody *Nelson Mandela*!'

Jonathan lowered his paper slightly and gave me that look (his mother's withering look we knew so well). He was about to tell me off, angry at being distracted, when he caught sight of the famous figure approaching, hand outstretched.

But the hand wasn't for me.

To my eternal surprise, and dismay, Nelson Mandela ignored me with my big smile of recognition, eager to meet my hero in this most unlikely of settings, and went straight for Jonathan. Half dropping his paper, Jonathan's hand shot up to shake that of the man who we, like so many others, had talked about for years, admired from afar. A legend. Jonathan did his usual thing when caught out unprepared: he sort of mumbled something that only I understood to be kind, respectful, quietly delighted – amused at the strange little twists and turns of life.

Nelson smiled then swept around and made for the exit.

It was all over so quickly that we had no idea why of all the people in the lounge – in the world – Mr Mandela had picked Jonathan. Why would you do that? Why would you pick a man buried in his newspaper, caught completely off-guard? Why would you ignore the excited woman by his side?

Why not me?

Was it because I was a woman?

I tried not to dwell on the thought.

I didn't like being ignored but somehow I had come to expect it. Jonathan, typically, thought that Mandela was having a chuckle by approaching someone who wasn't paying attention. Jonathan always saw the best in people.

Later, we were to find out that Nelson Mandela was there to meet convicted terrorist al-Megrahi, who was being held in a prison in Glasgow for the Lockerbie bombing. Mandela was an official observer making a visit to ensure that he was being treated properly in prison and to persuade the authorities to let him serve out his life term in a Muslim country rather than in Scotland. Al-Megrahi had no one.

'It is a form of psychological persecution that a man must stay for the length of his long sentence all alone,' Mandela had said, knowingly.

What he made of events to come – al-Megrahi's release, Gaddafi's downfall – is difficult to imagine.

𝖧𝖧 𝖧𝖧

I was struck by how much of what Dee described resonated. How could all this information be gleaned from the set of compressed jagged lines on my chart?

She went on.

'You have a tendency to cut yourself off from others at various points in your life. This feature is very strong in your chart, Kay. Is this the way you tend to function, the way you deal with the men in your life?'

Well, I had abruptly left my husband to live on my own. It also made me think about the time when I had cut loose from my musical background almost as soon as I started to work in London. After all those years of practice, all those scales and arpeggios, exams, lessons at the Academy of Music, years of study and degrees, I suddenly dropped it all. It was a huge disappointment to my husband – he often asked me to play the piano that we had bought from Mrs Sloss all those years ago up in Scotland that had been with me ever since – it travelled everywhere with me – carried lovingly up and down flights of stairs as it was moved from flat to flat and house to house. It stood there now, black varnished wood, cold white notes, abandoned, silent at the side of the room that we rarely used. And yet, to me, it was fine, it made sense.

I wasn't going to be a professional musician. I would always enjoy music but I wouldn't be playing in orchestras or attending lessons to sit exams or to perform in competitions. I'd be using what I had learned – creativity and musicality – to help me move on and develop new skills.

The more I thought about it, the more I realised that cutting myself off had become a constant theme in my life; family – a year after Mum died, instead of continuing to pick up the reins as some expected, I instinctively pulled back; work – always moving on enthusiastically to the next challenge, the next career change, never looking back; there was the divorce – suddenly cutting myself off from life with my husband and our beautiful house in Scotland.

꧄꧄ ꧄꧄

The house we bought was Grade II listed. It was a detached red sandstone villa built in 1856 on the Clyde coast with views across to the Arran hills; it had been my sanctuary. I'd loved being close to the water, the ferries, the birds, even the occasional grey seal.

We had bought the house with the intention of returning to live in Scotland one day.

'Don't go back to Scotland just to be near your parents. I know we are close to them and it's great to be with them but they won't always be there,' my husband had said, prophetically.

It was Mum who first went to visit the villa – it was only fifteen minutes away from their house – and rang me to describe its tower, sweeping gravel driveway and a plot of land at the side big enough to build a tennis court. It had once been the summer residence of merchants down from Glasgow accompanied by their staff.

Mum approved so we bought it and built an indoor pool, renovating the rooms one by one. Little did I know that one day it would all be abandoned – including furniture, paintings and pictures brought back from our travels to hang in the rooms. Somehow I never quite got round to sorting things out.

Dee looked sorry for me.

'I can see more transformation coming in your life over the next few years, Kay. You are on the cusp of dramatic change and are ready to leap into the unknown – that is what I see in your chart.'

'Before I go,' I replied, 'I have a question for you. Right at the end of the birth chart, you write about planets being in Sagittarius at the time I was born but it doesn't say much about my star sign Scorpio.'

Dee looked very surprised.

'You're not Scorpio, you're Sagittarius, Kay, quite definitely.'

We laughed.

All my life I thought I was Scorpio. I knew I was on the cusp, but I had no idea that you had to look closely at the detail.

I called my ex-husband to tell him.

'Guess what? I'm Sagittarius, not Scorpio.'

'Really?' he said, and then, 'I want my money back then,' trying to be funny.

But beneath his bluff was a sadness. I once told him that he was my 'perfect partner' according to a magazine article about horoscopes and compatibilities. It said Cancer and Scorpio were two of the most perfectly matched signs in the zodiac.

You see, sweetheart, it's perfect, it was meant to be!

Jonathan would give me long, well-worked out arguments as to why astrology was just hocus-pocus. The population couldn't be reduced to zodiac signs, he said, but still went along with it and smiled because it seemed to make me happy.

Now curious, I began looking deeper into what this shift in star sign actually meant. It had always been a little hard for me to see that I was a typical Scorpio – all those deep, dark, intense qualities, the strong passion and desire, the tendency to be manipulative. I tried very hard to find all these traits in myself and usually managed to convince myself they were there – ah yes, of course!

But now, when I looked at Sagittarius it all suddenly fell into place. Yes, here were traits I could identify with: independent, a bit feisty, slightly wild, adventurous, fun-loving and friendly (outwardly) and determined to live life to the fullest. A life built around the search for meaning and purpose. Wasn't that what I was doing now, embarking on this punishing programme of physical and psychological torture so that I could discover greater meaning? Taking everything to the very limit?

Over the coming months, I would have other charts done – transit charts looking at my next twelve months and what was in store. Dee suggested I also try the new digital versions that you could order online. There was even a chart that the hugely successful British astrologer Jonathan Cainer prepared for me (hmmm), giving me daily readings and planetary activities likely to affect me during changes in the alignment of the planets. I loved his encouraging, philosophical style, even though it couldn't possibly have been personalised for me – it was as though it had been produced by a computer and after a while I even began to notice repeats, which was a bit disappointing.

However, I was hooked.

Each day I would read my daily message from Jonathan Cainer and try to connect whatever was written on the page with events at work or my love life. It wasn't straightforward, but I liked working things out – I was sure it meant something.

To my surprise, once I started talking to friends about my chart, they were keen to have their astrology charts done too (even those who didn't believe in it). Dee ended up doing charts to give away as presents. And, although I had charts done by other astrologers, Dee's remained the most insightful.

I later found out she'd spent hours working on it because she had wanted it to be as accurate as possible.

The experience of working with Dee made me think about things in a new light. Rather than punishing myself for what I had done in the past, I could see how my actions and character traits had been affected by how I was brought up, my parents' outlook and circumstances. There was no blame but I began to understand myself a little better.

PS I've since discovered the 'catastrophe' on the day I was born. Apparently the nurse in the hospital managed to slice off the whole tip of my nose. My mother was absolutely furious when she saw the painful gash on the end of my little button nose (would have been good for Red Nose Day!) – she was worried I would be scarred for life.

As Dee predicted, I got over it.

32

'As each limb was pressed, massaged, eased back into shape, every piece of me would find itself taken care of'

Massage had become a constant in my life. It was like a best friend; a therapy I grew to rely on whenever things got on top of me. The combination of physical touch to ease tight muscles and stiff joints with no talk and often a little gentle music provided the perfect antidote to the stresses and strains of working life. I couldn't see the point of babbling on when you had such a perfect opportunity to shut yourself off and escape from the outside world. I'd come to realise I was ready to have a spiritual existence. Life was not just a matter of rushing around, pounding the pavements, piling up more and more to do. It was important, I'd learned, to just 'be'.

My spiritual side was emerging and growing and it was a very personal, solitary journey.

卌 卌

I'd come to know some of the therapists well – I became a regular client and gladly spent a good amount of time and money with them over the years. I'm still in touch with quite a few today and go back for sessions now and then.

I've had sessions all over the world, in spas, hotel rooms, on retreats, at Champneys, in Skyros, at Relax.

Styles ranged from formal to casual – there were sessions with women dressed in white starched tunics or men in T-shirts; there were massages on the beach in your bikini and chair massages with you fully clothed. Hot stones to deep tissue, aromatherapy, sports or Thai massage. Was it with an Indian head massage? Did you want reflexology or reiki? Did you want thirty minutes (rarely), sixty minutes (only if ninety minutes not possible) and where would you be before and afterwards – relaxing area, tea at home or swiftly ushered out to make way for the next waiting client?

There were the heated beds, hard fold-up mobile beds, stiflingly hot rooms, freezing cold rooms, heavy towels, light sheets, floaty light duvets, wool blankets or mats spread out on the floor. There would be music – classical, New Age, Indian, Native American, Chinese, Japanese, whale song, birdsong, lapping waves, Peruvian pan pipes or water fountains.

And not forgetting the oils, which ranged from cheap coconut oil to the most expensive, made-to-order blends chosen according to your needs – relaxing lavender, uplifting geranium, rejuvenating frankincense, bergamot, orange, lemon, rose, cedarwood or a potion with a tiny amount of each. There might be a 'sensory' test – dabbing different oils on your hand first and allowing you to choose a scent that appealed to you. The idea was that you'd be drawn to the scent that you 'needed' most that day – sporty citrus, calming rose and geranium or restorative lavender.

'Ah, you must need help with fitness and energy today,' she said.

Whereas next time, I was told, 'Your body must need to rest today, so after the massage, just relax and have a warm bath with candles later. And drink plenty of water to remove the toxins released by the treatment.'

These days when I start with someone new, I can immediately tell if the therapist has just finished training or been practising for a long time, even whether they are right for the profession; whether or not their heart is in it. It is an art form. Those therapists who love their job are a godsend and you're always in for a treat as they know how to use the many different styles available to them and can adapt to their clients' needs – there's pummelling, effleurage, kneading, tapping, gentle pinching, even elbow circling to relax any knots or tight areas on your back.

〽〽 〽〽

Bridget's massage was strong and brisk with lots of generous splashing of oil (good for dry skin and when you're in need of an energy boost). It was quite easy to feel like a filleted fish by the end of the treatment, but you'd always leave feeling revived after she'd unblocked all those 'congested' areas and stimulated the blood circulation.

Carlotta was Italian, very experienced, and worked at Space NK in Notting Hill. She had a spiritual aura, having spent time living in an ashram. After showering and changing into the fluffy chocolate-coloured bathrobe and slippers, I would make my way upstairs where candles flickered gently in alcoves as I moved along the cream-painted hallway, zigzag walls on both sides. Therapists glided down the long corridor dressed in angelic white, speaking in hushed tones and offering herbal teas and lemon water to the guests. Daylight streamed in from a window above. There were books to browse through as you waited – covering everything from photography to yoga, art, design, nature and beautiful gardens of the world.

Carlotta often had her favourite music playing as I entered the treatment room – 'Grace' by American singer-songwriter Snatam Kaur, who had studied New Age Indian devotional music. Carlotta would choose rose oil for me – a favourite scent that boosts self-esteem, mental strength and can help counteract depression – just what I needed.

Plants in a set of four test tubes on the wall and scented candles shimmering in glass bowls set the scene.

We'd talk briefly before the treatment began – romantic issues again – but didn't dwell on them. I'd lie face down. Carlotta would cover me with a towel. Her hands moved slowly from feet to calves, to thighs, sides, then back and shoulders, pressing down gently as she 'awakened' each area, ready for the massage. She'd then peel back the top cover to reveal my back and for the next twenty minutes she'd concentrate on my neck, back and shoulders.

Tears were not uncommon as my week-long build-up of tension eased.

Carlotta seemed to genuinely care. It was a simple transaction, a meeting of minds through touch; a temporary escape from the world. In a whisper, I'd be asked to turn to the other side for the second half of the treatment – moist cool pads were placed over my eyes and the treatment would resume. As each limb was pressed, massaged, eased back into shape, every piece of me would find itself taken care of.

At that moment I was complete, my best self.

I'd relax until I heard the sound of Carlotta striking Tibetan prayer bells together just once to signify the end of the treatment. Then she would leave, closing the door silently as she went.

Now alone, I'd take a huge deep breath, open my eyes and look around the room, taking in the music, the candlelight, the warmth. Totally content to be in the moment.

Ning's Thai massage, in contrast, took place in a curtained-off area at the back of a nail salon. Here, the walls were covered with religious paintings and there was a tiny shrine with fake flowers, incense and a gold leaf Buddha. Ning's Thai massage qualification had pride of place in a frame on the wall. Before starting, she would rattle off a quick little Thai prayer to ask for wholeness and health to be brought into the body, she'd then put hot towels on each of my feet in turn and knead my toes, ankles and heels. The intense massage would begin, using Tiger Balm – a heady mixture of camphor, menthol and clove.

Ning was small and nimble and from time to time, she would stand upright on top of the bed, legs placed either side of mine, holding my arms behind my back in different ways, stretching and curving my spine, then letting go. Occasionally, she'd press down hard with her feet or upper arm on my thigh muscles and calf muscles, restricting the blood flow in the groin area for a few seconds before releasing. I would feel blood surge through my veins, re-oxygenating, bringing warmth and energy back to my body.

At times it was very strenuous, and I'd find the sessions quite challenging. At the very end when I was lying limp, almost asleep, exhausted, Ning would lean in and tap my shoulder ever so gently with her fingers.

'We finish now, Kay. How you feel?'

Jessica saw clients at her home. I'd visit her at weekends. She would greet me in her tunic with a watch fob on her top pocket to keep an eye on the time, like a nurse. She'd mix lavender essence and massage oil together and prepare the room before I arrived. It was warm and comforting. After the session, we'd have a chat over a cup of tea and a piece of cake. She was one of the therapists to whom I became close. Whenever she hadn't heard from me in a while, she would start to worry and text me to check everything was OK and to see when I was coming back.

I could tell when it was time to move on.

Sometimes it became too close for comfort, the relationship became awkward when I felt the therapist knew too much about me and I felt unable to retreat into silent anonymity. I didn't want people getting too close.

I was afraid they'd find out that I was still unable to fix my problems.

After a few months I had a full contact list of psychotherapists, coaches, healers, therapists and spiritual 'helpers' on which to call.

Music, my first love, was an important part of all these treatments. Once you became accustomed to the music played by a particular therapist, you'd begin to relax the moment you heard the first note. Conditioned as you were to let go, it was the signal to drift off, thoughts and images swirling through your mind.

Yet sometimes I wouldn't be able to relax and would lie with my face stuck in the massage bed hole, studying the therapist's feet moving around from one side to another. Stripy socks, bare feet, nail varnish, toe rings, white tennis shoes, even fluffy slippers.

Occasionally I would have a bad experience. Once when the music sounded like someone sloshing about in a bucket of water (none of your gentle trickling over pebbles in a brook) while ships blasted off their foghorns in bad weather.

And I was cold.

You *have* to be warm – massage hands need to be warm and comforting, not like icicles, and the oil is always best warmed up – it helps absorption into the skin and the release of its scent. Sometimes it felt as if the therapist was warming their hands up on my body – thanks a lot – miserable when you're naked and paying.

33

Before I was made redundant, the company I worked for was good at ensuring that staff had help with professional development. I'd asked for some coaching rather than doing any more formal training courses and was lucky enough to be sent to an experienced Irish coach called Nick.

Nick played an important role in my path to emotional recovery.

Our sessions together were revealing. Not only did they delve into the psychology of work, my motivations (and those of others) and looking at ways of dealing with the complex issues in the workplace, such as politics and people, but he taught me how to deal with so many different personalities and inevitable conflict. Nick focused on problem-solving and tactics to help me change outcomes and questioned my usual approach – an approach that had worked well in the past but was now hitting obstacles.

It didn't take long before Nick and I realised that many of my issues stemmed from a range of deep-seated beliefs established early on. We focused on these and, in time, what began as professional coaching became life-coaching.

Yet once we had reached a certain point in our discussions, he recommended trying a healer he knew to work through my outstanding emotional issues; that healer, in turn, would recommend another healer who worked more deeply 'at the cellular level' but that was much later.

And so off I went to see my first healer, Martina.

34

I didn't know it at the time, but not only was Martina a craniosacral therapist or 'healer', she was also a dancer, an acrobat and a qualified yoga teacher. For an Italian, she was calm and inscrutable. I enjoyed her sessions after work – an oasis of calm following a hard day – she listened and understood and for many months I went along every week. I later joined one of her fabulous yoga retreats at a farmhouse outside Pisa.

Later, I'd find myself watching a YouTube clip of Martina doing acrobatic dancing with her partner. There, suspended from the ceiling between two enormous red ribbons performing an aerial duet was Martina in a bodysuit of shiny black leather, black tights and high heels. I watched as this beautiful figure slowly twisted and turned like a contortionist in a mid-air tango set to accordion music. It was pretty erotic stuff. A bit of a shock though – after all, she was my 'healer'.

For the most part, Martina and I would sit face to face in armchairs discussing the latest turn of events in my life – the various demands of work and family, the relentless pursuit of 'something'. I'd then lie on her massage table, she'd put on some restful music and begin.

What did she do?

The funny thing is she didn't really do anything. Yet it always surprised me how much better I felt after the treatment. Her treatments involved placing her hands on different parts of my body in turn: my head, my stomach, my solar plexis, squeezing her hands gently under my shoulders, under my back and my butt (I'd roll over slightly to make space).

It was a complete mystery to me what she was doing but it seemed to relax the different areas and was deeply calming and warm wherever she touched (perhaps not surprisingly). She would position her hands and leave them there for five, sometimes ten, minutes at a time. My stomach would start to rumble and growl – I wondered what was happening but trusted that it was doing me some sort of good. As with so many therapies, it was about energy being channelled into the areas that were out of balance or 'depleted' and helping you let go of anything inhibiting good health. Martina was helping draw energy to the places in my body that needed healing most, especially areas of what therapists like to call 'dis-ease'.

Sometimes my anxiety was so severe that even Martina couldn't shift it and after a full hour of healing treatment, I was still so worked up and panicky inside – that paralysing panic that sometimes takes hold – that we could still see my solar plexis pumping away.

Finally, after one such episode, Martina decided to send me to see another healer, a woman called Isabel who, she said, 'worked at the deep DNA level'. The idea of going even deeper appealed, not just because Martina thought I needed a more robust approach, but because I was happy at the prospect of another new experience.

᛭᛭᛭ ᛭᛭᛭

Isabel was an older lady, very experienced, who practised out of her home in Ruislip. She had her own treatment room at the side of the house with anatomical diagrams on the wall, shelves of books on therapies and a plastic skeleton hanging in the corner.

My first 'deep' healing session was pre-empted by a chat. I was wondering how it would compare with seeing Martina.

For some reason our conversation turned to the Olympics. Isabel told me she was working with a team of healers on problems with the Olympic site – they had identified problems with the stadium and were working on regular healing sessions together to help resolve the issues, which, over the course of my several treatments, apparently succeeded. I was fascinated by what sounded like white magic.

'So what are you worried about?' she asked.

I told her about my sessions with Martina, my active solar plexis and panic attacks that were increasing in frequency. She wanted to know what I thought caused them. That day I was annoyed with one particular colleague who I had been told was enjoying the attention he'd garnered mainly as a result of my own company's work in the Olympic legacy.

I wished it didn't bother me but it did and I couldn't do a thing about it.

At the end of the session, Isabel made a few notes on my card.

'You know you needn't worry about him, that man at work,' she said, scribbling. 'Everything will be resolved and you'll get your just desserts, he won't be a problem.'

I was relieved, if a little guilty, to have made such a big deal about it. But a few months later I remembered her comment. We were in an Olympic Borough meeting when one of the group suddenly disappeared from our planning meeting, only to return a few moments later, ashen-faced. He'd had some terrible news. The man I had talked about had suddenly died. He'd had a massive heart attack.

A coincidence, maybe, but still it made me wonder.

35

'Sounds like the oldest one in the book if you ask me, Kay. He's not a bad man, he's just a very indecisive man'

I jumped on the phone and selected, 'Next available reader,' rather than going through the rigmarole of speaking with the operator service, then going through all the psychics who were free that evening and arranging a call at a set time.

I was put through immediately.

A stern voice at the other end of the line said, 'Hello, I'm Maria – who am I speaking to?'

'Hi, Maria, I'm Kay.'

'And what can I help you with tonight, Kay – your love life, health, family issues?'

'Love life,' I said, cursing myself (had I ever asked for anything else?).

༄ ༄

Out of the blue, I'd heard from 'him' again. It was a shock. I didn't want to respond. I reminded myself how it had played out – the excited phone calls, in the early days, full of fun, which suddenly ceased, followed by the truncated, brusque or even angry exchanges by email or text towards the end. All he'd had to do was send or answer a text and I was like a little lap dog trying to jump up on his knee to see if he'd give me some treats or a pet.

He was his old suggestive self.

'Ah, do you remember Congleton? It was great, Kay.'

What was the point?

𝍸𝍷 𝍸𝍷

'So what is it that you want to understand about your love life? Is there something specific going on?' I drew a deep breath.

'Yes, I was with a man. He's back in touch after a long time. I've been moving on with my life and slowly getting there.'

'OK. Aren't there other men you could meet?'

'Yes, but I thought you could help with some insight.'

'What does he say to make you think things will be different this time?'

I was silent, knowing there was nothing.

'Sounds like the oldest one in the book if you ask me, Kay. He's not a bad man, he's just a very indecisive man. This isn't going anywhere.'

Maria went on, 'You have to be a lot more steely in your dealings with people, particularly men like this who will lead you a merry dance and, if you're not careful, they'll completely destroy your self-esteem. The reason I say that is because I see someone else in his life, did you know about that?'

The automated voice cut in:

'You are nearing the end of the call – if you want to continue with your reader, press 2, if you want to end the call as planned, you have two minutes left to finish your reading. I'm returning you to your chosen reader.'

I didn't press 2. That was all I needed to know.

'So, Kay,' Maria continued, 'is there anything else you want me to look at for you?'

'Anything I should know about relating to my work?' I said, half-heartedly.

'Well, the picture here is much more positive. You are already a successful lady – is that correct?'

'I suppose so.'

'What area of business are you in?'

'Media.'

'Ah, that explains it, in the area of communications and working with others you have some talent and you are set to do good things. If you don't allow yourself to be distracted, you won't have any difficulty there, you'll sail through and triumph in the end. You seem well positioned so it shouldn't be hard. What is it that you are doing?'

'Working on the Olympics legacy.'

'Ah, that sounds like a big project. You just need to toughen up, be strong and keep your eye on the prize and everything will be fine.'

'Thank you, that's encouraging.'

'Kay, you need to forget that man right now – he's not interested in anything long-term. Don't let him rain on your parade.'

Click, the line went dead.

36

'This man is free, he has no baggage, he wants you. He's been through a lot and is trying to establish a relationship with you'

Elsa worked as a psychotherapist at an alternative therapies clinic only a few stops along the DLR from my studio flat at Canary Wharf. She was the first psychotherapist to challenge me directly. She was German and spoke English with a slight accent; she was direct (ouch!), organised (lots of neat notes), punctual (always on time, almost scarily to the second!) and slightly cold to begin with. There was no messing about. She questioned everything I said. Perhaps she sensed that I was strong enough to take her style of investigation – no longer the sad soul with extra baggage.

Rather than letting me talk, Elsa led the sessions. I liked her approach. She made me think.

I was in the honeymoon period of a new relationship, and already plagued with doubts.

'I'm having trouble trusting Graham,' I said. 'He's quite private, enjoys time on his own and doesn't always talk. In the past I did everything together with my partner, we talked incessantly and I never doubted what he thought and often felt I knew what he was thinking.'

'Yes, but that's the past, Kay. Everything's different now.'

'But after the Egypt guy, I don't think I'll ever be able to completely trust a man again.'

'Everyone's different. You're obviously happy with Graham, so what's the problem?'

'Sometimes he disappears or goes quiet and I feel uneasy about that, as if something's not right, as if he's hiding something or doing something he knows I won't approve of – it's just a sixth sense, nothing concrete. Although I'm often right – it's only later when I find out where he's been and who with – out with friends from work, meals, drinks, coming back late. I don't understand, why does he do this?'

'Maybe you push him into it. Have you ever thought about that? All this constant monitoring of what's going on, who he's seen and what he's done, what he's eaten, exact precise details. Perhaps it's just the way he is, and he doesn't want to share everything with you – the way you were used to before. And remember, if a man – anyone for that matter – wants to do something, anything, no matter what it is, whether it's some hobby, drinking, going to a prostitute or just having some time with friends away from their partners, they will find a way of doing that if it's what they want. Can you see that?'

'Yes, I suppose so, but I thought we were getting close enough by now that I'd know more about him, know his every move.'

'Does he know about you, about "your every move" as you put it?'

'No, I suppose not. I don't always share – well, sometimes he's not interested, and if I don't volunteer information he doesn't press, and if he *is* interested and asks me a straight question I'll answer. But if it happens the other way round I rarely get a straight answer, it's always half the story that I want; he makes me feel as if I'm prying.'

'I think you are. Don't people have a right to their own thoughts? Don't people have a right to some space? And don't you want the same? As long as you feel good around him isn't that all you need?'

'You're probably right but somehow I need more.'

'Ah, yes. Good old "reassurance". You're insecure. Maybe he doesn't trust you yet, have you thought of that? Look, you will never know what people are thinking – even if they tell you, as you've just said yourself, there are a lot of things going on inside that you might not want to share openly. You might not even understand your own thoughts fully, so how can you relate all these clearly to someone else? You have a right to privacy and so does he. Everybody does.

'The decision is really yours, Kay. Do you want to be constantly nervy, focusing on him and what he's doing – and thinking the worst? Or do you want to trust him? You've already told me all the good things he does and that he often makes you happy – do you want to trust him and get on with living your life together and apart, having a healthy relationship that allows space to be committed but also to be interesting people in your own right? Surely that was the problem before and you needed some freedom to become more fully you, a more rounded person.

'This man is free: he has no baggage, he wants you. He's been through a lot and is trying to establish a relationship with you. You seem to be battling it at every stage, looking for issues. It's not a competition.'

That struck home.

I'd been looking out the window as I considered this and then looked back across at Elsa. Her words seemed critical, but her demeanour was soft and kind.

My three sessions with Elsa were enough to give me a big push to make an effort to trust more and see where things led, rather than to be constantly analysing, something she said might lead to trouble.

37

'When I emerged from the session, guided back to consciousness, I felt lighter, brighter and more positive'

As soon as my head touched the pillow, my mind would start racing. As a solution to my insomnia, I'd started buying audio recordings to aid relaxation, otherwise known as guided meditations, or a form of self-hypnosis. There's a bewildering range of these audio recordings on offer and at first I found it very hard to choose. There were so many different approaches (a walk in the country, looking inside yourself, off into outer space, religious). There were male versus female voices to choose from, all with different accents from different countries.

Eventually I found a male voice I liked – not too posh, but middle of the road, which meant I wasn't distracted. The last thing I needed was someone who made me giggle, someone whose delivery was overblown, hackneyed ('your path in life', 'wherever you go, there you are') or overly emotive with breathy background music.

The voice on this recording was quietly powerful – deep and convincing – he sounded as if he was sitting on the sofa next to you, talking naturally; as if he'd done this a thousand times before. He spoke slowly and clearly. It was very enjoyable listening, enabling me to relax easily.

Once I had listened to this recording several times over a period of some weeks, sometimes on a daily basis, I began to anticipate every word, every change of scene – the garden, opening a gate, walking over grasslands, picking flowers, observing the sounds, the birds and the blue sky. Safe and secure, it was dream-like, and it worked.

When I emerged from the session, guided back to consciousness, I felt lighter, brighter and more positive.

And most nights, I slept like a baby.

38

the group listened silently, staring blankly at me, their faces sort of dead, unmoving, as I went on describing the ridiculous efforts I was making to "sort things out"

I read about alcohol dependency and that it might be passed down through the generations. Both my father and my grandmother were adopted and so I knew very little of their family history. And, although I wasn't aware of it in mine, I couldn't help but wonder as my father struggled for a time. Now widowed, and becoming increasingly frail, he lost his faithful canine companion, Kauri. Coming, as it did, just a few years after Mum died, it was particularly harsh and took its toll. We tried to persuade him to get a new dog, perhaps a rescue dog, but no, he'd made up his mind. He didn't want another dog and with it, the inevitable pain of loss again. Every one of his dogs had lived a good long life but each at some point had to be put down when it was decided that it was no longer fair to keep it alive. So once again, Dad held his dog close, looking into its eyes, stroking its head and talking gently as the vet did his job. I was with Dad this time and he said Kauri knew – it was so sad.

My mother had died a few years before, and my father still couldn't comprehend why he'd been left behind. He had made good provision, expecting Mum to survive him as most women do, and she'd be well provided for. For her to die first baffled him. He had cared for her every step of the way over a four-year period as she gradually became more and more weak. It was a full-time job. Now, living alone, he fell into the role of grumpy old man with nothing to live for. Afflicted by failing health, he became an old salty sea dog, smoking too much, drinking too much and watching too much TV (even his beloved David Attenborough programmes weren't always enough to keep him happy). He was sad and miserable.

Living and working in London, and dealing with my own midlife crisis, I had missed his rapid decline. I hadn't visited for months and when I did eventually see him, I was shocked by the transformation. He would rant about the state of the world, and at night release terrifying screams, reliving horrors from his time at sea – he had once seen a man gunned down in front of him. Sleeping in my old room with all its happy childhood memories, ornaments and trinkets, old soft toys and pictures – a strange experience – I sat bolt upright. I couldn't sleep with the shrieking downstairs. My father had always given me support, hope, everything I needed, and now it seemed it was my turn.

At first, I didn't know what to do, so I started by making changes to help involving social services, family and friends. Ultimately, this phase would lead him to writing his incredible life story – Jonathan and I quickly realised helping him write his memoirs would be beneficial and the whole family embraced the idea. We hoped it would reconnect him to friends and help others to realise what a wonderful life he had led, that there was so much more to him than the grumpy old man some saw.

But for the moment, I was running around trying to stop him smoking and drinking too much, and although I didn't know it at the time, I was making things worse. My decision to attend an AA meeting myself was in desperation – to see if I could understand the 'problem' and change the tide.

Attending my first AA meeting was a challenging experience. Instead of patting me on the back for all the things I had been doing so diligently, the group listened silently, staring blankly at me, their faces sort of dead, unmoved, as I went on describing the ridiculous efforts I was making to 'sort things out'.

I'd arranged for the redecoration of his house, bright clean surfaces replacing the nicotine-stained paintwork. I moved him downstairs, re-did the bathroom, installing a new walk-in shower, grab bars, new sinks, underfloor heating, a new oven and hob. I was running around confiscating bottles, emptying the overflowing bottle recycling bags from the outhouse, cancelling large orders from the winery of 'The Visconte di Bertolucci de Toscana' and pouring away the gin and cokes hidden in unexpected places. I was trying to focus his mind on the new project, positive changes, anything to stop the rot.

At the end of my story, I could see that others were sympathetic. There had been nods from the group. Some looked away or down at the table, perhaps reminded of their own stories. I found out that none of my descriptions were a surprise. They had heard it all before. They had been through it themselves. They shared a common bond and I was just another victim of an experience that was far from unique.

The most important thing I learned in these sessions was that I was doing all the wrong things. The more I tried to 'help', the worse the drinking would become. My rushing around was pointless. I was just making it worse for everyone else, especially my dad, and, more importantly, making it unbearable for myself. I was exhausted. I was upset. Nothing I did improved the situation. I wasn't helping anyone.

Alcoholism is an illness. It's not curable. All you can do is abstain and that's not going to happen unless the person wants to stop drinking. It's their choice, their free will. You must either accept or act – and you can only act if the person wants to stop. It's their life, their choice and who are you to tell them what to do? We all have our own way of dealing with tragedy and loss, of dealing with death – an inevitable fate we all have to face. You can't judge others, and, yet again, the message I still hadn't learned – the only thing you can change in any situation is yourself, your own attitude. You can't change others.

'Ach, I don't give a bugger,' Dad would mumble.

For a time he was really low, and his ailments were really getting him down. I should have been more understanding.

My friend Daisy said, 'Kay, he's over eighty, we'll probably be like that too some day. If I was him I'd take a drink to cheer me up and get me through the day. It must be hard no longer being able to do everything and being alone.'

AA was invaluable in allowing me to see things from a new perspective. Gradually I began to approach things differently and to see that I was so far from perfect myself, and certainly in no position to judge anyone else. My own 'escape' was therapy – obsessively trying everything. Therapy was my crutch and as soon as I stopped over-functioning around my dad, things began to improve. It was a gradual process but, in time, a degree of acceptance and understanding replaced indignation and embarrassment.

At one point, my father ended up in a geriatric unit for fourteen weeks after a fall – he was miserable and couldn't wait to get out. Once home, he vowed to himself he would reform otherwise he'd be back in there 'with all the loonies'. He did it. All by himself.

39

'Her delivery was as matter-of-fact as if she was describing making a cup of tea but I caught, "gently insert", "rectum" and, to my relief, "removal of toxins"'

The 'hydrotherapy' centre was round the corner from my flat and I passed it every day on my way to work. Catching sight of the staff inside in their starched white outfits, I was curious. It looked professionally run, which you'd want if you were going to have a 'colonic irrigation'.

I'd never tried anything like this before and was naturally a little apprehensive. But eventually I worked up the courage to go and sign up for a session. Gosh, it was expensive, even by my standards (my mounting monthly therapy bills were always a shocker) but as it was such an intimate treatment I felt it must be worth it.

I wanted to see if it could help me find some sort of equilibrium. To my mind, it was just another route to 'cleaning out' the past to make way for the future.

As usual, there was a long questionnaire to fill in about my general health. After looking through my answers, the therapist confirmed the information I had scribbled down about my skin (dry), my digestion (mixed), how much water I drank (not much, mainly tea), my sleep patterns (on-off) and what I wanted from the session (she looked a little surprised at my response and made a note at the end of the form – probably 'mad one').

I was then treated to a long list of the benefits – everything from helping with medical conditions (including cancer – really?) to flushing out body toxins, eliminating fatigue, helping you lose weight, and providing a quick route to looking great – eyes, skin, digestion could apparently be transformed and you'd most likely end up with the elusive flat tummy. Super. Of course the best way to benefit was to have a course, not just a one-off. But I wanted to try it once, first, before committing to any more sessions.

The treatment room was warm, dimly lit, with a bed, white towels and a machine with tubes and knobs making a continuous humming noise. The description of what was to follow was toned down and the therapist was using language that was as non-threatening as possible. Her delivery was as matter-of-fact as if she was describing making a cup of tea but I caught 'gently insert', 'rectum' and, to my relief, 'removal of toxins'.

'No, thank you, I don't want to see the "result", I said. But, 'Yes, it would be good to know what you think it tells you about my system.'

'A healthy colon equals a healthy person,' she announced finally, as she started with the procedure.

The treatment was as gentle as you could expect – with a tube inserted into your backside. The therapist was young – very young (had she left school early to start cleaning out the nation's unclean, I wondered). She gently massaged my abdomen and stomach during the session as it rumbled away as if something was coming to a simmer inside. She was quiet but if she noticed me looking uneasy, as if to say 'what was that?' or 'is that a normal gurgle?' then she picked up again, explaining how it was cleansing the colon and intestines very softly then flushing out the same area with clean or purified warm water at just the right temperature for your system.

I tried to take my mind elsewhere, but I was keen to find out the results and, as long as it wasn't too painful just uncomfortable, I was happy to go through with the session.

Afterwards I rested in the relaxation area and was advised to take it easy for the rest of the day. I had a nice bath that evening and waited to see the miraculous effects on my eyes (should be brighter) and my skin (should be clearer). I found evidence of improvements, but I was far more interested in the fact that I was being cleansed of my past and psychologically, I was moving on from a feeling of being 'stuck'. I believed it helped and was happy with that. Somehow I knew that one session was enough: I didn't need to have ongoing treatments.

卌 卌

Later, when I talked to my healer, Isabel, who seemed to know about such things, she told me not to pay a fortune for cleansing treatments but to do it myself.

'It's just an expensive "enema",' she said.

Enemas date back to biblical times and have been used regularly for cleansing in many cultures. Isabel showed me the bits and pieces you need (a plastic bucket and a tube) and where to buy them and gave me a two-minute explanation of the DIY version, emphasising the need for absolute cleanliness throughout the process. She recommended a version using warm coffee (not decaf!) as caffeine aids digestion. These can be done weekly, daily or even several times a day, depending on the patient's gut (!).

I tried it a couple of times but stuck to warm water – coffee seemed a bit too much for my squeamish self. (This is the girl who fainted at a school careers convention where in the medical section there was a plastic body laid out with its entrails on show. Thud, down I went.)

No, best keep it simple.

Eventually I decided that, although I'm sure there are real and important benefits to internal cleansing, for me, colonic irrigation felt too harsh. I threw the paraphernalia out. There were far more pleasant treatments on offer. Taxi!

40

'I believed in the need for women to be more in touch with their nurturing selves — especially someone like me who had an upbringing with very little physical contact'

As usual, it was a friend who recommended I try Esoteric Breast Massage (EBM).

'What's "esoteric" about it?' I said.

'Well, I think it's like a "club" of people "in the know" compared to people outside the club who know absolutely nothing about it.'

Hmmm, a bit like the Masons then, great!

Not entirely convinced, I asked a few more questions but each time she just said cheerfully, 'Best to go and experience it yourself, it'll ruin it if I try to explain,' or 'I'm not the therapist, just a client, but it's fantastic, life-changing. And I think you'll love it. You're a strong woman in a male-dominated industry and might benefit from reconnecting with your feminine side.'

Gawd, it sounded terrifying, but she was probably right.

I was intrigued. It sounded a bit of an odd one though and I have never really been comfortable with anything to do with my breasts. I'd even go so far as to say they had been a bit of a nuisance throughout my life, too big for my liking and, as a younger girl, I used to draw in my shoulders to hide them. They seemed to be important to men, but left me self-conscious and uncomfortable. As a woman, I didn't really have any use for them as I'd never had children, only checked them for lumps now and then, and for me, they were never about physical pleasure. But hey, my friend knew someone who she had been seeing for a long time and so I decided to try it out. Maybe it would awaken something in me.

When I went to see Lyndsay, I loved the way in which she introduced me to her world; she explained the background to esoteric healing more generally. It was a system developed in Australia that took a special approach to physical and mental ailments, in which human interactions were nurturing of the individual. Typically, during surgical operations the doctors, nurses and their theatre teams would prepare by creating the best possible environment – this involved restful, meditative music, deep, slow breathing (often with the team in sync) and choreographed movements. If the patient was not sedated, they'd participate in the breathing ritual to bring the whole group into perfect harmony; connected and conscious of the important part relaxation should play in delivering positive results.

Thankfully, I wasn't having a surgical procedure.

The room was very warm (like a 33°C hot yoga session) and, although it was cold outside, I was soon able to undress without rushing to get under the blankets. Lyndsay spoke quietly, unhurriedly, and said it was an important part of the session that I don't feel pressured or uncomfortable. 'It should feel like being back in the womb.'

For some time, she stood at the top of my head and massaged me – everywhere else but my breasts – massaging in long soft strokes down my back and around my torso, my stomach and particularly down my sides to my thighs. She explained that the treatment was to help women to reconnect with their body, that by being more aware of their breasts and feelings connected with them, they would experience their innate gentleness more profoundly. By the time she eventually began to massage around my breasts and nipples, I was slightly less self-conscious, more accepting, I had let go – a little.

Now, to be honest, I didn't really like the focus on the breast and because I didn't feel different – not emotionally moved in any way – afterwards, I felt as if I'd failed. Either I couldn't let go fully or, subconsciously, I didn't want to. Either way, it wasn't really for me so after a few sessions I stopped.

For years I'd viewed my physical self as separate to the rest of me. I was a workhorse, physically and spiritually quite shut down. I appreciated Lyndsay's efforts and respected her beliefs.

It wasn't for me.

Yes, I believed in the need for women to be more in touch with their nurturing selves – especially someone like me who had an upbringing with very little physical contact. We weren't a particularly tactile family and as a result, physical bonding had been neglected. But, sadly, in my mind, my body was there to get things done, a tool to enable things to happen – to transport me to far-flung places, to work hard, to be fit and healthy, forcing the last ounce of energy out of my system to get on.

41

'cupping has become a "remedy" for almost every type of disease — as well as a complimentary treatment for muscle fatigue and general relaxation'

Remember the Olympic swimmers with those painful round marks across their backs? Yes, we'd all read about cupping and, although the procedure sounded (and looked) painful, I thought it worth a go if, as reputed, it could remove 'toxins' responsible for 'holding you back'. Once again, the treatment had been around for thousands of years, courtesy of the Africans, the Greeks and the Chinese. While originally used to suck out the toxins of snakebites and skin injuries, using the hollowed-out rounded end of animal horns placed on the body, cupping has become a 'remedy' for almost every type of disease – as well as a complimentary treatment for muscle fatigue and general relaxation.

Round the corner from my flat was a small Asian medicine centre that advertised cupping in the window. The pictures showed a smiling blonde lying on her front, bright-eyed, her face resting on thick, fluffy white towels with four even-ly-spaced, detergent-clean glass cups on the middle of her back. Orchids bordered the image and she looked relaxed and comfortable.

Inside was a little different. Everything was a little the worse for wear – the glass cups weren't the cleanest – black marks from constant 'firing', the white fluffy towels were thin and grey, and I wouldn't at any point describe myself as relaxed or comfortable. No music, flowers or pleasant scents – the therapist looked a bit scary, certainly workman-like (in a 'shifting rubble at a building site' kind of way). In fact, first impressions and the cold treatment room (she was still wearing her padded coat!) might have been a deterrent, but given my determination, I wasn't going to be put off.

(Note to self: perhaps research more thoroughly before enthusiastically plunging in? Ah well, too late, let's get on with it.)

After a gentle (ish) massage with (cooking?) oil, the therapist prepared to whack on the cups – all six of them. I could hear her lighting the taper and turned my head to watch as she started pushing the taper inside each glass to create the vacuum necessary to suck up the skin into the 'bulb'. I couldn't exactly feel the skin being pulled into the cup – it was an odd sensation – but there was a definite tightness around the contact points as she dropped each one into the desired position – plop, plop, plop. She motioned for me to turn back and so I looked down through the face hole of the massage table and tried to enjoy this new sensation.

Next came the cups being moved around on the surface of my skin, pulling it away from my body to stretch the muscles rather than the usual downward pressure of conventional massage. She continued with this for a couple of minutes and then left me alone for another ten minutes to let the cups do their job. When she returned the cups were yanked off and she rubbed my back with a couple of hard paper towels.

Ouch.

Was that it?

Apparently so.

As I dressed, I turned to look at the rings on my back – they looked 'angry' and a bit black and I was glad I hadn't opted for the more advanced 'wet' cupping treatment where they pierce the skin with a needle before applying the glass, thereby 'bleeding' the area. Positively medieval and not for the faint-hearted. It took a week for the marks to disappear.

42

'The energy will go where it's needed most, whether that's spiritual, mental or physical'

While working at the BBC, I became a regular at the on-site hairdressing salon. Getting your hair done is therapy – a cessation of work, a chance to relax and be pampered – and with any luck you'll look and feel better, ready to resume your day refreshed. The BBC hairdressers were responsible for the haircuts, trims and styling seen on most of the personalities and newsreaders you find on TV.

It was great to have somewhere so handy given that the BBC offices were a little isolated out at White City. You could nip down from the office and be done within half an hour and enjoy a chat and a cuppa, with the added fun of having celebs popping in too. When the BBC took over new offices slightly further away but still within walking distance of the main building, we moved into the sparkly new complex. One of the best BBC stylists, Madeleine, took the opportunity to open her own salon beside the new development – and I followed her.

Madeleine was primarily involved in running the hair salon but over time, added new services to her business. Talented and extremely driven, she ended up doing everything – tanning, false nails, waxing, facials, make-up – the works.

During my regular shampoo and blow-dry we'd always have a heart-to-heart. I could always trust Madeleine to give me good advice on what to do with my hair. She'd try to balance my growing impulsiveness ('Why don't we cut it all off?' or 'I'd like to dye my hair a deep bronze colour – what do you think?') with the practical needs of my work and life. The wall posters were brilliant for giving you ideas; I stared at the model looking wistfully over her shoulder with perfect straight blonde hair right down to her waist; another showed a stunning brunette wearing a see-through chiffon gown, her chignon interlaced with flowers (it was actually taken in Madeleine's back garden in West London with borrowed pot plants).

Madeleine knew I was keen to make things happen in my life – she was sympathetic but she also knew I was making rather a lot of hasty changes and perhaps experimenting with too many new things so she thought it best to have some stability in the hair department. Typically, I usually left with a well-maintained, neat and business-like hairstyle.

Over time, we became close; I was in her salon twice most weeks, occasionally at weekends for longer appointments to have a cut or highlights. Consequently, Madeleine knew all about my interest in alternative therapies. And so, when she too became interested, I was one of the first to be offered a free session in reiki. Madeleine was training to become a qualified reiki practitioner and had to find people willing to be guinea pigs. I was happy to oblige.

I didn't know anything about reiki so I just turned up and waited to find out.

Here I was in the treatment room surrounded by hot wax boilers, nail colour charts, false eyelashes, hair colour samples, bottles and jars of creams and gels and serums and a tall, shiny, black all-over spray-tanning booth. Ready for reiki.

Madeleine finished with her last client of the day.

'Right, all set, Kay?' she said as she closed the door behind her. 'All you have to do is lie down and relax,' she added, eyes sparkling. 'Leave everything else to me.'

'Like this?' I said, fully clothed.

'Yes, keep all your clothes on, well, apart from your shoes and remove all your jewellery and that belt – anything that's tight or constricting – you need to be completely comfortable. OK, up on to the bed and lie down flat,' she said, patting the treatment table.

It was warm and Madeleine put on some gentle chanting. I lay down on the padded massage table. A new scent was added to the 'toasty' smell of spray tan. Madeleine flicked a lighter several times, finally igniting what looked like the ends of a bunch of dried-up grass about six inches long. She placed them in a copper dish and was now trying to extinguish the flame, blowing it softly.

'I'm burning sage. It's one of the most cleansing herbs. It opens the chakras and gets rid of negative energy.'

'Does it help with being fed up with men too?'

'Ha ha, probably yes,' Madeleine squinted over at me, smiling as she tried to blow out the last bit of flame from the deep red and orange embers in the copper bowl. 'It's good for anger and depression and it cleanses the body of bad spirits.'

'Well, I certainly need to be cleansed of bad spirits and help with the removal of anger,' I said, smiling back, though it was far from funny.

Madeleine was relieved when the smoke started to rise.

'It isn't always sage, you can burn cedar or juniper too but I like sage and it's really good for emotional purification.'

Reiki, another therapy that's thousands of years old, involves the medicinal burning of herbs otherwise called 'smudging'. Although it's been used for centuries by Native Americans, Ancient Greeks and Romans, not to mention the Ancient Egyptians as a way to cleanse, it was the Japanese who used it to heal 'soul energy' and gave it the name reiki (the Japanese 'rei' is from soul, 'ki' is energy). That's the therapy as it is known today, which even purports to boost the immune system and cure illnesses.

Madeleine picked up the bunch of smoking sage and walked around me, a trail of smoke encircling my body. I tried not to giggle. Thankfully, the strong, smoky scent forced me to take in a long, deep breath and relax. It soon erased all the other smells (and thoughts) and began to fill the room. I drifted off, eyes half-shut, as Madeleine placed her hands close to my body, not yet touching, just hovering above.

From the corner of my eye I watched as she began to 'scan' through my body, starting above my head and moving down past my face and neck so that I could feel the warmth of her palms as her hands passed over. Then past my shoulders, heart, stomach, legs and finally, my feet. She came back to my stomach and solar plexis.

'I can feel the energy here is a little weak. Your chakras are all in need of a little work, but I'll spend more time on these two areas.'

She placed her hands on my stomach. 'This will help the energy flow into these areas.'

I imagined a flow of positive energy and felt something change, a gentle pressure. My stomach started gurgling and where, before, there had been an uncomfortable pumping sensation (my system overworking), I felt things slow down and become calm.

I closed my eyes.

The last thing I heard Madeleine say was, 'The energy will go where it's needed most, whether that's spiritual, mental or physical.'

The next thing I knew I was out, in a world of dreams, not unlike the guided meditations I had been listening to at home.

When the session was over and I'd opened my eyes, I felt energised and positive, looking forward to the rest of the day.

Madeleine gave me a short summary of what she had found (weak heart chakra – not a surprise) and off I went.

I was reminded of my healing sessions with Martina, where the touch was quite firm. Reiki seemed much subtler, but maybe it was just Madeleine. I was sure she'd succeed as a reiki practitioner. She told me the key was learning how to channel energy through the top of her head (the 'crown' chakra) and chest (the 'heart' chakra) and then sending it on through her palm chakras to you.

Over the years, I did a few more reiki sessions but I always preferred craniosacral healing, which to me is a stronger therapy than the gentler reiki. At the time, I felt I needed more to spur my system into action.

The funniest thing I ever read about reiki is that it can apparently 'heal' animals too. They enjoy the experience and may even 'show' their appreciation after treatment by licking, sighing deeply (!) or giving the reiki practitioner 'a look of appreciation'. Not so dissimilar from us humans (besides the licking), then.

43

From astrology and birth charts, it wasn't too much of a leap to become fascinated in numerology and the idea that 'your numbers' – calculated from your date of birth – influenced your personality. The more you knew about yourself, so the thinking went, the more you'd be able to enjoy and appreciate each day, and perhaps influence outcomes.

I'd first seen a book on numerology while waiting for a massage appointment – I took down the information and went off to buy a copy.

As with any of the 'methods' or 'therapies' I tried, you had to have a willingness to believe. I felt I approached each one openly, believing it could help. I never discounted any method as each provided some sort of window on my life, not always at the time, but sometimes many months, even years later.

With numerology I followed the process carefully and looked up what the numbers meant, keeping them safe to refer back to later.

Wherever you look for information about numerology, up comes Pythagoras, the Greek philosopher and mathematician who is at the heart of it all. He couldn't stop looking for meaning in numbers and eventually went further and found a way to use numbers to give insights into people's personalities, their lives and futures. Although it's interesting to delve into the history of Pythagoras, so much is unproven that I found it a bit of a maze and I struggled to find out if the insights that the numbers revealed were real.

However, I got to work calculating my 'numbers' by adding various bits of my date of birth 22/11/1957 (according to the instructions), so that I had my Day Number (defines your personal characteristics), my Life Number (defines your life path) and Present and Future Numbers (defines developments in a specific year). In each case I had to add up the numbers, continually reducing them until I had a single number. I couldn't wait to know what the numbers actually meant.

My Day Number (4) was easy – I just added together the numbers from my day of birth 2 + 2 = 4

A '4' person is a great builder and has the ability to transform dreams into reality. Sounded good to me!

Next, I calculated my Life Number (it's 1) by adding together all the numbers in my full date of birth, including the month and the year:

$$2 + 2 + 1 + 1 + 1 + 9 + 5 + 7 = 28$$
$$2 + 8 = 10$$
$$1 + 0 = 1$$

The Life number (or birth force) gives you a life view of your personal characteristics over many years. For me, a '1', it's in my nature to be a pioneer and get on with things, occasionally throwing caution to the wind. It seemed to fit.

I calculated my first Future Number (2) in 2012 by replacing my birth year 1957 with 2012 and following the same process – it would give insight into my experiences in that particular year:

$2 + 2 + 1 + 1 + 2 + 0 + 1 + 2 = 11$

$1 + 1 = 2$

So 2012 was a '2' year.

Once I had the numbers I looked up what they meant. My 2012 description fitted perfectly – a focus on cooperation and partnerships on every level (Olympics legacy work), negotiation featuring strong and personal relationships becoming closer.

And just for interest I calculated my Future Number for 2020 (it would be a '1' year which seems to look at new beginnings and new people, there is focus and independence, clarity and energy, but also a testing year – let's see).

For 2019, it wouldn't be quite so good – rather mixed in fact. It would be a '9' year, which means travel, loneliness and jettisoning all that doesn't work for me (cutting myself off again?), which leads to some feelings of insecurity.

Given how easy it is to get the numbers wrong, I had to check them several times. But I found it compelling once I'd started and was amazed by how many endless possibilities there are once you start to look at the different years or your best partner compatibilities, what characterises you at work, your personal traits and what you were like as a child. I needed to make sure I wasn't seeing this as anything other than a helpful insight, a pointer, something thought-provoking rather than being exact. But soon I found myself looking up other peoples' fates – I just needed a date of birth. Addictive.

More complicated scenarios arise when you try to work out how all the different numbers (and traits) of the Day, Life and Future numbers interact with each other, especially when conflict arises. For example, my Day number suggests a practical consideration of outcomes before jumping to conclusions whereas my Life number suggests I'm quick to react. There are endless ways to look at what the numbers mean in relation to you. It was fun, and something to refer back to, but ultimately, although fascinating, it was complicated and required more time than I was willing to devote.

44

'As she placed each card down on the velvet she'd either contemplate silently or immediately articulate what she was "seeing", what the cards were "giving" her'

I was introduced to spiritual or 'power' cards on my yoga retreats, usually as a fun after-dinner activity. It offered a new world and a new way of thinking, and I was surprised by how many people seemed to use them routinely in their daily lives. I was immediately drawn to the idea that these cards could change my perspective and stimulate confidence and optimism.

Apart from tarot (the 'queen' of cards) there were many other sorts of decks, including angel cards, goddess cards, power animal cards, all beautifully produced and illustrated with booklets describing how best to use them.

At first I wrote them off as religious claptrap; New Age, hippy-dippy, a little 'witchy' but that was to deny their breadth and complexity. They were constructive and a useful tool for positive thinking.

I'd started attending Mind Body Spirit and Psychic festivals. Here, I'd noticed 'readers' holding their decks close and wouldn't let anyone else touch them as it could alter their 'essential energy' – they were personal to the reader; the cards were larger than playing cards, good-quality but well-used, even slightly frayed at the edges. These people were clearly long-time 'users' and believed in the power of the cards. I was always struck by how kind they were, generous with their 'gifts' and keen to help others through their insights. They tended to speak slowly and modestly.

I always felt encouraged and supported by their readings.

One tarot reader who I paid to see at the Olympia festival offered to do another reading for free and emailed me out of the blue a few months later as he'd had some time to look at what was in store for me. He used the Native American cards and produced a reading, which I found intriguing, but difficult to understand at first – the language can be quite strange and assumes a great deal of knowledge and acceptance.

I was reassured when he explained that the Death card was not one to be afraid of – it can have many interpretations depending on where it appears and in relation to what subject – love, family, work. For me, it often signified new beginnings – death of the old, opening up to the new. He also mentioned the Raven, my 'power' animal that signifies transformation.

During one of my previous guided meditations, I remembered seeing a Raven hovering and circling high above a burial ground. They're frightening birds – in Greek mythology, they're associated with Apollo, the god of prophecy, and often seen to be a symbol of bad luck. But the reader told me that the raven represents change and is associated with mischievous and curious people with a sense of humour.

'If you are seeking spiritual rebirth, this is the "power animal" to invoke,' he said.

'When you walk with the Raven, be prepared to go deep into the realm of the unconscious towards your true self. It will bring long-lasting healing for mind, body and soul.'

It seemed to fit, if rather fanciful.

I especially liked what is probably the most recognised set of tarot cards – the Rider-Waite deck – bright colours and haunting illustrations. I bought a small four-by-three- inch pocket reference book, the Bible, and began carrying it around with me for inspiration, mainly at weekends when I was alone walking in Hyde Park, listening to music and stopping for tea and a read. I knew the cards needed to be respected to get the best out of them, and I didn't trivialise them.

However, I was also being constantly told that everything was 'as it should be', my 'fate' was sealed and I should 'go with the flow'. So if that was true, my little 'tarot Bible' would always show me whatever I needed to hear at that moment. I could trust it. I began to have fun with the deck and played Russian roulette with my little book to see where it led; I'd sometimes just flick through until I wanted to stop and read the page I'd stopped at or else I'd shut my eyes and open the guide randomly at a page as if cutting the deck. Then I'd read the selected page and would often find that it revealed some-thing about my situation that would cause me to reflect.

I often found uncanny connections between what I read on the page and what I wanted to know. I'd be thinking about how things were going to turn out after this 'phase' was over (at first, I thought it would be just a matter of weeks or months, not years). I wondered if I would ever feel settled again, or as successful as I had been before – would the upward path return?

I opened a page at random – it was The Emperor.

The Emperor was sitting on his throne, long beard and crown, dressed in metal armour like a medieval knight. It said, 'Success is just around the corner but elusive; you must be patient, you fear that the support of father/husband/ partner/significant other may not be there'. You could ask a question or send a message at any time then wait for the answer to 'come to you'.

After using the Angel cards, sometimes I'd invoke the 'angels of finding things' (if there is such a thing) if I lost something precious – usually very quickly I'd retrieve the lost object. Sometimes I'd just say to myself, 'All is well, all is as it should be,' to calm myself down if I woke up in the middle of the night – again, these were reassuring phrases from the cards.

Danielle practised out of a hotel on Baker Street – yes, the very same Sherlock Holmes hotel as before – pure coincidence (I think) – a friend had given me her number after she'd had an intriguing reading with Danielle at home. Danielle was multitalented and not only did tarot readings but massage too so we'd cover both 'therapies' during one session. She'd open up a silk drawstring pouch and pour out the contents onto a velvet surface: charms and crystals, pink and opalescent gems, a tiny Buddha and other items of spiritual significance – including a strangely shaped piece of twig (!).

She would shuffle the cards and ask me when to stop (sometimes I thought hard about what I wanted to know about and took several seconds to respond, other times I was pretty muddled in my thinking and stopped her quickly and randomly). She'd shuffle several times during the session and, on dividing the deck in two, asked me to choose. (I wasn't allowed to touch her cards for fear of altering the 'energy' of the deck.)

The next stage was quite invigorating to watch – she very quickly placed the cards in a pre-determined line and sequence. To me it looked confusing – some cards would be placed in a line one below the other in a single long column, then Danielle would start another column about six inches to the left, then create another in the middle. Little piles of cards would sometimes spring up at the outer edges of the main spread. As she revealed cards from the top of the deck, they would carefully be laid in place to create a whole picture of what was going on.

As she placed each card down on the velvet she'd either contemplate silently or immediately articulate what she was 'seeing', what the cards were 'giving' her.

'Ahh, your relationships are settling now. I see two men in your life and they are both good.' (I hadn't said anything about my relationships beforehand, best not to pre-empt.)

'Does that sound right, Kay? Are there really two? Well, these men are both there in different guises, and it all seems positive – look, the sun there, it all looks bright with those other cards around it – they are quite powerful cards and no pain, no swords, no waiting.'

It is said that you can't pick the wrong card as the law of attraction means that you'll always choose the correct cards to match the energy or vibration of the question you asked.

When I worked with cards on my own, occasionally I'd fumble when shuffling and certain ones popped up or jumped out of the pack; I was told these cards had special meaning and were not to be ignored. I'd read their meaning with interest.

There were always uplifting messages, restoring confidence, but I also knew in my heart of hearts that this couldn't go on. I needed to get back to reality. I couldn't live in this shadowy, spiritual world forever. I had to get a grip.

At the end Danielle said, 'You don't need to see me any more – it's all a pretty picture for you now and although you'll have to work very hard, it's paying off.'

45

'I sat there reflecting on my situation. After years in the wilderness, I was back in the real world, my midlife crisis left far behind'

Today I followed the coastal path, not another person in sight, alone with nature. My partner Graham dropped me off to walk the five miles and would be there to meet me at the other end. The sea was calm as the sun began to drop behind the cliffs. The clouds were lit up in deep pinks and greys and, looking across towards the beach, I noticed wild lupins growing up through the pebbles.

It took me back.

These lupins had pushed their way up through the stony surface. Now they were tall and strong. I reflected on the parallels with my own journey. Once trying and difficult, it had eased up. I was more settled and stable, thanks to the decisions I'd made.

It was mainly thanks to the therapies – and therapists.

Earlier that afternoon, as we drove down to the coast, we were discussing a message I'd just received from a friend. In it, she recommended I try a detox diet for my muscle pain. It had worked for her. In fact, I often received texts, pictures, Facebook posts and emails from friends offering advice, or sending on inspirational quotations or proverbs. I liked this regular flow of positive energy. I recognised it as something that had now been part of my world for a long time, over a decade.

Graham was baffled.

'I don't understand why your friends are so keen on sending these sorts of messages. They happily pass it on as if it were important. Idiotic. Who cares?'

'Are you calling me an idiot?' I said through a smile.

Ping. Another text:

Key to a good life: If you're not going to talk about some-thing during the last hour of your life, then don't make it a top priority during your lifetime.

I scrolled back through some others.

There was Ingrid Bergman: *Success is getting what you want; happiness is wanting what you get.*

And, *Whatever women do they must do twice as well as men to be thought half as good. Luckily, this is not difficult.*

Eckhart Tolle was in there too: *When you do something, you should burn yourself up completely, like a good bonfire, leaving no trace of yourself.*

I didn't like them all but I loved that one. It reminded me of how I approached my long list of therapies, racing through the experiences, hair flying, fanning the flames, no holding back.

'Why don't they just get on and deal with it themselves without bothering everyone else?' Graham said.

I burst out laughing.

'You just don't get it, do you?'

Actually, most men don't. It's a woman's world – this world of encouragement, confidence giving and support.

How is it that after all this time, women are still struggling for recognition, bright little girls, subdued, oppressed, restrained or silenced by the male figures around them as they grow up? After centuries of repression, it's no wonder that they've woken up wanting to rebel and find their voice.

'It's just another form of therapy, a support network,' I tried to explain.

But Graham was intent on his driving. He didn't get it, and why should he? He was a man who had been through a lot and dealt with it in his own way. That was his way. He simply didn't see the point in involving others in the mess.

He was fatigued by the exertions of the holiday, a sprained knee and the gloomy thought of returning to work. He was disappointed not to be enjoying our favourite walk together, but he knew it would make me happy so here I was.

At the halfway point, I sat down on the bench and listened to the birds. Rye Harbour Nature Reserve has hundreds of birds nesting or visiting the beautiful marshland made up of miniature lakes and islands. At different times of the year, you can see ducks, terns, avocets, sandpipers, grebes, egrets and cormorants drying their wings and sometimes flocks of birds swarming and swooping high up into the sky. We came here often. It made us feel happy to be alive. Watching the gulls overhead, flapping their wings and falling backwards awkwardly as they dropped shells onto the shore, I was interrupted by a text.

It was from Jonathan, always positive.

Great event 400 children and we sold quite a few books – they seemed interested in the new game too.

Our business had settled down after a few false starts and was now beginning to take off. We were always in touch, working on new projects, gaining expertise and establishing a team. There was an enduring bond.

I sat there reflecting on my situation. After years in the wilderness, I was back in the real world, my midlife crisis left far behind.

All those therapies I'd tried. What did it mean?

Each had given me something, had made me think differently, feel differently or behave differently. I'd discovered reasons why things were as they were in my life.

I had learned so much.

I knew about alternative medicine – it had taught me how to cope with problems and how to be self-sufficient. I had made new friends and now had a more spiritual dimension to my life.

Like my ideal man, outlined in precise detail in my NLP session, I'd wanted someone 'well-rounded' and whole. That's what I'd become. I'd had adventures along the way – what life is all about.

It was getting dark so I pulled my hood up and zipped my fleecy jacket as I set off on the final leg of my walk.

Despite the many 'predictions' of astrologers, psychics, tarot readers and what's in the cards, I learned that life is about choices, and how you respond to your childhood and life experiences. It's also about timing: you have to wait and see: you can't rush life. I've stopped trying to pin down the facts before they happen. I'm not trying to control the uncontrollable aspects of my life any more, nor am I trying to control those around me. We're all different. I'm just grateful to have jumped in at the deep end and survived.

I'm still that little girl in the wild lupins but I don't need to hide any longer. I only wish I could have told my six-year-old self what an amazing time lay ahead, and for her not to be afraid.

GLOSSARY

1. ACUPUNCTURE:

A therapeutic treatment from ancient Chinese medicine in which fine needles of various lengths are inserted into the skin at specific points around the body. Up to twenty needles may be used in a single session, and they may also be connected to a low-voltage electric current. Acupuncture is based on the belief that illness and pain can occur when the body's essential energy ('Qi') is unable to flow freely around the system and that physical injury, emotional stress or infection are potential causes. The placement of needles stimulates the body's own natural healing response and helps restore a healthy energy flow. In my first treatment, I found myself pinned down, naked with a chain-smoking 'doctor' with not a word of English and unfortunately, little or no insight into my midlife crisis, but I persevered.

2. AFFIRMATIONS:

If you believe in the power of the subconscious mind to create change and that *'you are what you think'*, then affirmations are for you. To enable change, we must first define our thoughts, then develop relevant affirmations and ultimately create actions in order to 'manifest' our intentions. Affirmations can alter the dynamics of our brain so that we truly begin to believe that anything we want is possible. Affirmations strengthen our intentions, but be careful what you wish for … one of my 'dreams' came true.

3. ALCOHOLICS ANONYMOUS (AA):

Long-established global organisation first set up in the USA in the early 1930s. It offers a twelve-step process to help recovery in alcoholics and is based on supportive group sessions that take place in a safe and 'anonymous' space. AA is open to alcoholics, their families or friends. The whole ethos is non-judgemental – something that's often difficult, especially in today's open and opinionated world.

4. ASTROLOGY:

Astrologers study the positions and movements of the planets in relation to each other at particular points in time. For millennia people have believed these celestial movements can help predict events and human behaviours and complex interpretative systems were developed in many ancient civilisations. Astrology provides a potential insight into an individual's personality and events during their lifetime. Providing a precise time of birth (to the minute) allows an accurate 'Birth Chart' to be prepared by plotting the position of the planets at the exact moment of birth. Astrologers use the chart to make interpretations about you, your life and relationships. Daily readings specially produced for an individual can also be supplied by qualified astrologers. These tend to be more insightful than the brief horoscopes you read in some newspapers.

5. AYURVEDIC MEDICINE:

Ayurveda is a form of complementary medicine and one of the world's oldest. It originated in India thousands of years ago and is, to this day, one of the country's most traditional methods of healthcare. It uses herbal remedies and special diets combined with other health-giving treatments such as massage. Many retreats in India offer ayurvedic holidays in comfortable, sometimes luxurious, resorts.

6. BIOMAGNETIC PAIR READING:

A treatment using pairs of magnets placed in and around different areas of the body to help equalise the pH balance of the whole system.

7. CARD READINGS:

Organised in terms of the different types of card decks (tarot, goddess, power animal, angel). The individual cards are often beautifully decorated. Typically, an experienced 'reader' will lead the interpretation of each person's character and life experience, either done in a group practice, or individually. They can be insightful, beneficial and can change your thinking.

- **Tarot:** A fortune-telling card deck reputedly originating in Europe in the 1400s. Card sizes and designs vary, but are often larger than playing cards. There are five suits: wands, trumps, swords, cups and coins, with cards featuring signs and characters, such as The Magician, Emperor, Hanged Man, Wheel of Fortune and Justice. It's a joy to watch an experienced reader carefully setting down the cards, one by one, then explaining what they mean for your future. It's the position, orientation and adjacencies of the cards that determine the meaning.

- **Goddess Cards:** These feature a range of different goddesses that can help with family, health, relationships, finances, career or other problems. Decide on a question, focus on the question and the cards will deliver an 'answer' that is supportive and designed to guide you to positive action. The cards are beautiful objects in themselves, high-gloss and exquisitely designed.

- **Power Animal Cards:** Connect with your 'animal spirit guides' using this set. They can often support you with your life choices and provide insight into your personality. My power animal turned out to be a bird – the Raven, which is associated with curiosity, fun, mischief and transformation. It's fun simply looking up what each animal stands for. If my power animal had been a horse, then I'd have no problem jumping the hurdles of life.

- **Angel Cards:** Each 'Oracle' card delivers a message from your guardian angels. If you ask for help with a situation, the angel that appears in the deck will help move you forward with calming and encouraging thoughts. If you want to use know-how to connect with your 'angelic power' there are instructions so that you can use the cards for others as well as yourself. It helped me keep calm after panic attacks. I would invoke the 'angel of finding things' if I lost something. It always worked though I'm not sure there's any such angel.

8. COLONIC IRRIGATION:

A hydrotherapy used to remove toxins from the body via the intestine, colon cleansing dates back to ancient Egypt. It's like an enema, but uses far greater volumes of water. Practitioners say it has many health benefits including weight loss, increased energy, brighter skin, softer nails, a flat stomach and can even improve psychological wellbeing. I was looking for a total clear-out of mind and body so was keen to try, but it's not for the faint-hearted.

9. CRANIOSACRAL OR HEALING THERAPY:

Can be helpful in reducing panic attacks and erratic moods common during the menopause – it's a gentle, hands-on healing that focuses on evening out the rhythmic pulses of the nervous system. The therapy is related to osteopathy, which works on skeletal structure and promotes wellbeing by working on the craniosacral system of membranes and fluids that surround the brain and spinal chord.

10. CUPPING:

This therapy uses heated round glass cups, which are placed on the body. The cups create a suction effect to help improve circulation. They can be moved across the skin during treatment, or left in place for some minutes, creating red ring 'imprints'. The therapy was brought to public attention in 2016 when it was used by the US Olympic swimming team. My experience was rather brusque and the angry red marks made me wonder – is this therapy? Then again, sixteen gold medals must mean something.

11. DERVISH DANCING:

A type of Sufi (Islamic mysticism) meditation based on a continuous whirling dance – the aim is to achieve a trance-like state of abandon, losing yourself and finding God through the performance of a continuous counter-clockwise spinning dance. It starts slowly and speeds up gradually over time. If you want to achieve an altered state of mind using just movement and music, this could be a good place to start.

12. DIAL A PSYCHIC:

A psychic claims to have heightened 'extra sensory' perception and therefore an ability to uncover facts and details about a person or events that are not evident through the normal senses. Psychics can be consulted by phone or in person and may use crystal balls or cards to help provide spiritual guidance.

13. DINNER DATING CLUBS:

A way of meeting people in a friendly, informal and unthreatening manner. Many different options exist but they usually have a regular published calendar of organised events. They are run as 'clubs' with the specific aim of providing the opportunity for members to meet dozens of interesting new potential partners in interesting surroundings. You'll meet lots of great new friends – mainly girlfriends!

14. ESOTERIC BREAST MASSAGE (EBM):

A methodology practised only by women, for women. Claims to be good for 'helping reconnect with your feminine side'. It's essentially a delicate massage that specifically centres around the lymphatic area of the breast. The therapy helps women become more aware of their body and – for those not good at checking themselves – more conscious of lumps or pain that may require investigation.

15. 'F**K IT' THERAPY:

A proprietary name. What started out as a remote Italian retreat for stressed-out professionals has now become a way of life for many who subscribe to the 'F**k It' philosophy. It's a tonic for everyday woes and an unexpected approach: jettison everything that doesn't work for you and simply watch what happens. The retreat was an escape from the grind with therapies on tap, beautiful surroundings and delicious food.

16. GUATEMALAN WORRY PEOPLE:

Traditionally South American. I was given a tiny balsa-wood box of handmade matchstick people to place under my pillow and was told that by the morning all my worries would disappear. The 'worry dolls' are mostly handmade of wire, wood or wool and are dressed in colourful, traditional Mayan style. The size of the doll can vary between half an inch and two inches.

17. GUIDED MEDITATION:

An easy DIY therapy to do at home. Simply pick your favourite voice and storyline then sit back and relax. Unless you're a total wreck, you'll soon be calm. It's essentially a meditative story, gently spoken by a trained practitioner and often accompanied by relaxing music to help calm the mind.

18. HOMEOPATHY:

An alternative medicine based on the premise that 'like cures like', but only using highly diluted substances (really only a trace) to aid natural healing. Practitioners treat the whole person, not just the symptoms, so they need information about lifestyle, diet and sleep patterns as well as state of mind. After a full analysis I was always prescribed a new remedy, a tiny pill, tailor-made for my situation at that point in time.

19. MASSAGE:

Innumerable types from many different cultures, each involving different kinds of pressure applied to different parts of the body by the therapist's hands, fingers, elbows or feet. The treatment should take place in a warm relaxing environment and is best accompanied by soothing music. Muscular pain is reduced, stress relieved and mental faculties rested and restored. If you like massage, it's the ultimate pick-me-up therapy.

20. NEURO-LINGUISTIC PROGRAMMING (NLP):

NLP is about personal development. First developed in the 1970s in the US, practitioners believe there is a link between language, behaviour and the nervous system and that changes can be made to a person's experience through careful re-programming. I diligently followed the plan with long lists of aspirations and visualising success. I wasn't convinced ...until a few years later.

21. NUMEROLOGY:

Using of a set of numbers calculated from your date of birth, numerologists believe they can outline personality traits and times of change in your life. Pythagoras was apparently the first to do this. I've mapped out my numbers for the coming years and look forward to seeing if it's true.

22. PAST LIFE REGRESSION:

Links to concepts around reincarnation, regression using hypnosis is a therapeutic and spiritual experience that takes you back to your memories of past lives. I still have a record of my first session. It led me to my most unusual midlife retreat in Egypt.

23. PATANJALI YOGA:

A type of yoga based on the ancient Indian sage Patanjali, whose wise words and approach are widely followed today. 'We're not going to change the whole world, but we can change ourselves.'

24. PSYCHOTHERAPY:

A widely used therapy to treat emotional problems or mental health conditions. It usually involves a course of one-to-one sessions with a trained therapist, talking through the issues in detail and allowing the patient to open up in a quiet, safe space.

25. QUANTUM THERAPY (QT):

According to the team of therapists that treated me, QT was first used to remotely check the health of astronauts in space. The 'Scientific Consciousness Interface Operations System' (SCIO) used churns out page after page of data as it scans the body for physical, mental and emotional vibrations. It records any imbalances and the therapists treating me used the results to suggest changes in my diet and lifestyle.

26. RE-EDUCATION:

This is one of many personal development programmes designed to bring about positive change to a person's life. It works by purging negative childhood beliefs that are holding you back. For some it is gruelling and diminishing while others feel liberated, more successful and able to move forward confidently.

27. REFLEXOLOGY:

A non-intrusive complementary therapy that can help improve your entire body system by manipulating key 'crunch' points on your feet. It's based on the theory that different points on the feet correspond with different parts of the body (organs, blood or nervous system). Face and hand reflexology is also performed but is less common.

28. REIKI:

A healing technique that channels energy to the patient by means of very gentle touch (sometimes the hands hover above the area without touching). A trained therapist works to reduce stress and restore wellbeing. Some reiki therapists burn herbs to help relax the patient and cleanse the energy during treatment. There is such a thing as Dog Reiki …

29. SHAMANIC RETREAT:

Shamanism is an ancient method of healing that believes emotional and physical problems are caused when our soul energy is out of balance. A shaman is able to see these problems and shift energy in such a way as to restore balance. Today there are many different ways to experience shamanism. My experience was with a group in Egypt – inside the pyramids, in the desert – an experience I'll never forget.

30. SILENT RETREATS:

There are many different types of retreat but they usually focus on a particular spiritual tradition (Catholic, Buddhist) and can be found in interesting places all around the world. Organised groups eat, live and meditate together in prolonged silence for several days. It can help to recharge from the stresses of daily life and work through uncomfortable past experiences, thoughts and feelings.

31. SINGLES HOLIDAYS:

Whether you want to meet new people, or simply don't want to travel alone, holidays for singles in groups are now very popular. You can visit almost any destination, try out a new hobby in the safety of an organised group or just do your own thing with the enjoyment of company at mealtimes and a group 'base' to return to each day.

32. SONIC THERAPY:

Sonic therapists use sound and music for healing. Our bodies are full of fluid and the frequencies within them can be altered by sound. During the therapy, a range of different sounds, from crystal bowls, gongs, chimes, drums or the human voice, are used to create healthy movement of energy around the cells of the body. Reducing dissonant frequencies relieves anxiety and stress and, as I discovered, can also heal past trauma.

33. VIPASSANA MEDITATION:

This form of meditation with its focus on the minute molecular workings of your body, breathing and circulation of blood has become a popular 'mindful' therapy. After ten-hour daily sessions, you can't help being in a meditative state.

34. VISUALISATION:

Achieving what you want in life may be down to your ability to visualise a 'new you'. Vision boards are often full of beautiful and successful people with endless money and fun. And because sometimes it comes true, it's very popular.

35. VOODOO:

An animist religion in which a person's spirit is believed to survive death and can be called on. Such spirits may also inhabit the bodies of others. It originated in West Africa and is practised in the Caribbean, where it brings together elements from Catholic ritual and traditional African witchcraft and magic. Communication with gods, ancestors and spirits involves trance-like states with charms, voodoo dolls, spells and spirit possession all common associations.

36. WRITING THERAPY:

Whether it's in the form of a private journal scribbled in snatched moments or as a more formal exercise to be shared widely, writing can be therapeutic as well as creative. Benefits include enabling the writer to appreciate what is important to them, to organise their ideas and have an opportunity to put issues and feelings into perspective. Many institutions and organisations offer courses – residential and non-residential – that can help hone your writing skills and connect you with other writers sharing their experience.

37. YOGA:

A group of physical, mental and spiritual practices originating in India that can be traced back many millennia. In Western countries in the 1980s it became popular as a form of exercise but it is important to appreciate that yoga has a spiritual and meditative core that can help practitioners attain a sense of inner calm and mindfulness. There are many different yoga methods and styles, so it is worth trying a number of classes until you find one that best suits your needs.

READING LIST

Aurelius, Marcus, *Meditations*, Penguin Classics, 2006

Byrne, Rhonda, *The Secret*, Atria Books, 2006

Coelho, Paulo, *The Alchemist*, HarperCollins, 1995

Dalai Lama, *The Little Book of Wisdom*, Ebury Publishing, 2000

De Mello, Anthony, *Awareness*, HarperCollins, 1990

His Holiness the Dalai Lama and Cutler, Howard C, *The Art of Happiness*, Coronet Books, 1998

Fein, Ellen, Schneider Sherrie, *The Rules*, Element/HarperCollins, 2000

Gibran, Kahlil, *The Prophet*, Penguin Modern Classics, New ed edition, 2002

Glouberman, Dina, *Into the Woods and Out Again*, Sphinx, 2018

Gray, John, *Men are from Mars, Women are from Venus*, HarperCollins, 2002

Hardie, Titania, *Zillions: Titania's Book of Numerology*, Quadrille Publishing Ltd, 2002

Harrold, Fiona, *Be Your Own Life Coach*, Coronet Books, 2001

Hay, Louise, *You Can Heal Your Life*, Hay House, 1984

Oken, Alan, *Pocket Guide to the Tarot*, Potter/TenSpeed/Harmony/Rodale, 1996

Parkin, John C, *F**k It: The Ultimate Spiritual Way*, Hay House, 2014

Peck, M Scott, *The Road Less Travelled*, Cornerstone, 1990

Taleb, Nassim Nicholas, *The Bed of Procrustes*, Allen Lane, 2010

Virtue, Doreen (Ph.D), *Goddess Guidance Oracle Cards*, Hay House, 2004

ACKNOWLEDGEMENTS

Grateful thanks to Chris Mulzer (Kikidan) for allowing me to share his insights in Egypt and to Dina Glouberman, who founded the retreats on the Greek Island of Skyros – my first retreat there was a great opportunity to reflect on life and a catalyst for change.

Thanks to Sony ATV for arranging permission to use an excerpt from the lyrics of 'The Dicky Bird Hop'.

'Dicky Bird Hop' Words and Music by Ronald Gourley and Leslie Sarony © 1926, Reproduced by permission of Keith Prowse Music Publishing Ltd/EMI Music Publishing Ltd, London W1F 9LD.

Affirmation material (page 80) taken from *You Can Heal Your Life* by Louise Hay (Hay House, 1984) reproduced with kind permission of the publisher.

Quoted material (page 79) taken from *Be Your Own Life Coach* by Fiona Harrold (Hodder Paperbacks, 2001) reproduced with kind permission of the publisher.

ABOUT THE AUTHOR

Kay Hutchison is a content creator with extensive experience in radio, television and publishing. After gaining her BMus and MA in music at Glasgow University she joined Decca Records in London and then BBC Radio as a Producer.

Kay moved across to television with Channel Four and went on to lead the launch teams for Disney TV and Channel Five. In the build up to the 2012 London Olympics she successfully led the legacy partnership that delivered a long term future for the multi-million pound Olympic Broadcast Centre.

Kay founded her own company, Belle Media, and launched Belle Kids in 2015 producing multi-platform, conservation focussed content for children.

An inveterate traveller with a restless mind her career is now centred around writing and publishing.

Find out more about RedDoor Publishing and sign up to our newsletter to hear about our **latest releases, author events,** exciting **competitions** and more at

reddoorpublishing.com

YOU CAN ALSO FOLLOW US:

 @RedDoorBooks

 RedDoorPublishing

 @RedDoorBooks